Reducing and Recycling Waste in Schools

Learning about materials and using them wisely

Ian Mitchell

Series Editor, Allan Randall

SOUTHGATE

First published 2005 by Southgate Publishers Ltd
Reprinted 2008

Southgate Publishers Ltd
The Square, Sandford, Crediton, Devon EX17 4LW

Printed and bound in Great Britain by
Imprint Digital, Upton Pyne, Exeter, Devon.

British Library Cataloguing in Publication Data
A CIP catalogue record for this book is available from the British Library.

ISBN 1–85741–185–4
ISBN 978–1–85741–185–0

Acknowledgements:
The authors would like to thank:
Clare Eastland, for editorial advice;
Ann MacGarry, Education Officer at the Centre for Alternative Technology, for advice on content.
Cover pics: Centre for Alternative Technology (centre, bottom left) LTL (top left, bottom right and top right).

Centre for Alternative Technology

The Centre for Alternative Technology (CAT) in Machynlleth, Mid Wales, is concerned with the search for globally sustainable, whole and ecologically sound technologies and ways of life.

Within this search the role of CAT is to explore and demonstrate a wide range of alternatives, communicating to other people the options for them to achieve positive change in their own lives.

We offer fun, facts and stimulating ideas, and cover various aspects of the curriculum, particularly in science, technology and geography for any level from infants to postgraduates.

Thousands of schools and college students visit every year and receive stimulating tuition, discussion and tours. Educational worksheets which complement the displays can be downloaded from our website.

We also produce publications for teachers and pupils and educational kits. For educationalists, we offer day and residential courses on sustainability, energy and using ecological footprinting.

For further information go to **www.cat.org.uk/education**
Tel: **01654 705983** or email: **education@cat.org.uk**

Learning through LANDSCAPES

Learning through Landscapes (LTL) is the national school grounds charity, whose vision is for children and young people throughout the UK to enjoy and be inspired by the unique opportunities and experiences that well-designed, well-managed and well-used school grounds can provide.

We advance the right of all children and young people to enjoy and benefit from their school grounds. This is achieved by undertaking research, providing advice, encouraging action and supporting all those who care about improving these important educational environments.

School grounds are special because:

- they matter to children, young people and society as a whole;
- they are the one external environment to which all children and young people have regular access;
- for some children and young people they provide the only regular experience of the outdoors;
- research shows that the design and management of school grounds can significantly affect children's and young people's development;
- they can provide unique experiences, opportunities and resources for teaching and learning in a safe and supervised external environment;
- they can be welcoming, stimulating, challenging and enjoyable environments providing a diversity of opportunities for fun, work, rest and play.

The benefits of school grounds

Evidence from schools shows that the benefits of well used, designed and maintained school grounds are wide ranging and considerable. At their best school grounds:

- **enrich** all areas of the curriculum by providing a unique and varied context for learning;
- **stimulate** motivation and curiosity, encourage creativity and help pupils develop a broad range of skills, competences, knowledge and understanding;
- **enhance** the appearance and richness of the area in general, support biodiversity and therefore contribute to a better quality of life for all.

For more information about Learning through Landscapes or to become a member and support our work, please contact us:
Mail: Learning through Landscapes,
Third Floor, Southside Offices,
The Law Courts, Winchester,
Hampshire SO23 9DL

Website: www.ltl.org.uk
Email: schoolgrounds-uk@ltl.org.uk
Tel: 01962 845811

Contents

Introduction

Reducing and Recycling Waste in Schools

This is a book for teachers. Through a programme of carefully selected activities the book will help children, aged 7–11 years, learn about materials and their properties. The activities are practical and fun. Each is presented by a cartoon rat with human characteristics. The rat is gender, race and age neutral, but has a deep interest in rubbish!

What does this book do?

It is a programme of activities that helps schools deliver part of the National Science Curriculum and at the same time promotes understanding of key issues for a more sustainable future, i.e. how we use and conserve materials, and, how we reduce waste.

Why do we need this programme?

The children are going to live their lives and share one planet with two or three times as many people as their parents did. Using the planet's material resources wisely makes practical, economic, social and moral sense.

Sadly compared to their peers in other parts of the European Union, many children in the UK grow up in a culture that is profligate and wasteful with the world's resources. Vast amounts of finite, irreplaceable material is either burnt or thrown away.

The programme helps children understand where the materials they use come from and what happens to them when they are thrown away. The topic is designed to help children acquire the information to make their own choices about how they use and discard materials.

Reducing and Recycling Waste in Schools should help to make your school a better place. For example:

- Children should develop a different attitude to waste and litter. These resources are often too valuable to be discarded and thrown away.
- The general school environment will appear more positive and conducive to good citizenship.
- The school will probably save money if it adopts a waste minimisation policy. In most Local Authorities the volume of waste thrown away determines how much your school pays for its waste collection and disposal service. The money saved can fund improved resources and staffing!

Household waste that is dumped in landfill sites:	
UK	81%
Sweden	23%
Denmark	13%
Switzerland	7%
Source: Green Alliance Autumn 2002	

On what is the Reducing and Recycling Waste in Schools programme based?

Many primary schools use the Qualifications and Curriculum Authority (QCA) guidelines to help them deliver the National Curriculum. This book is designed around the QCA Science Unit 3c *Characteristics of Materials*. The aims of this unit are for children to:

'…extend their knowledge of the range of materials and of the properties that characterise them. This knowledge should help them recognise what needs to be considered when a material is chosen for a particular use.'

Although this science scheme of work forms the backbone of this book, lessons that fit into other areas of the National Curriculum are also supplied.

These have been designed to fit into the Literacy and Numeracy schemes of work at an age appropriate level.

In addition, the National Curriculum states that schools should help children 'develop their sense of social justice and moral responsibility and begin to understand that their own choices and behaviours can affect local, national or global issues …' (PSHE and Citizenship guidelines)

The whole programme is designed to help schools meet this aim.

The activities in the book are manageable and fun.

Reducing and Recycling Waste in Schools has been written by an experienced teacher who understands what can realistically be managed in a busy classroom.

What the units contain

Unit	What the children will learn	Activities
1	To revise children's knowledge of materials and introduce the project.	A game identifying the material used being thrown away in a piece of waste.
2	To identify common materials and know that different objects can be made from the same material.	A classroom survey to identify objects made of specified materials.
3	To know the origins of many commonly used materials. To be aware that some materials are finite and others are renewable.	A quiz, using acquired knowledge, to determine the origin of some materials.
4	To recognise some of the properties of materials.	A database of the properties of materials used in of a variety of objects.
5	To understand that some waste materials are discarded in landfill sites.	A comprehension task, plus a word search, based on a newspaper article written for rats.
6	To know that in some cities rubbish is burned to provide heat and power.	A comprehension task, plus designing a poster, based on a newspaper article written for rats.
7	To learn that materials are suitable for making a particular object because of their properties and that some properties are more important than others when deciding what to use.	A structured analysis of the properties of a material used to make an object.
8	To understand that one of the properties of some materials is that they biodegrade.	Using a pictorial key to explain what will happen to various items of litter.
9	To create a test to see that worms remove biodegradable waste from the surface of the soil.	A diagram and explanation explaining a test that uses worms to biodegrade litter.
10	For children to understand that biodegradable waste can be collected and composted.	Answering questions and completing a crossword based on an 'agony aunt' letter to a rat.
11	To obtain evidence to test scientific ideas and carry out the test safely.	Planning and devising a test on a property of paper.
12	To experience and understand the concept of recycling.	Making a sheet of recycled paper.
13	To plan a test deciding what evidence to collect and to make comparisons and draw conclusions.	Testing the absorbency of different kinds of paper.
14	To know that many discarded items can be reused.	A mathematical activity based on information about 'clothes banks'.
15	To know that materials can be recycled and to know where to recycle them locally.	Interpreting a database on which materials can be recycled, and design a poster.
16	To carry out a survey of how the families of children in the class treat different kinds of waste material.	To record the survey information pictorially in a graph and suggest ways families can be encouraged to recycle more.
17	To know what can be reused or recycled and consider how to reduce classroom waste.	Devising a strategy for reducing waste in the classroom.
18	To plan a test to find out how strong an egg box is, deciding what evidence to collect.	Designing, making and testing to destruction an egg box for a single egg.
19	To increase awareness of how waste is produced or reduced.	To redesign the packaging for items in a school lunch box.
20	To revise and consolidate strategies for reducing waste and design a poster about this project.	A game followed by an activity to design a poster.

How to use this book

Reducing and Recycling Waste in Schools is easy to use. There is a set of twenty lesson plans, called 'units', to be used with primary children in Years 3–5. Each lesson plan consists of a 'teacher's page' and a photocopiable worksheet.

Teacher's pages
On each teacher's page you will find:
- A list of the objectives for the lesson;
- A list of the resources needed to deliver the lesson;
- Ideas on how the lesson could be organised and delivered.

Support material
In the 'Background information' chapter of the book are some of the basic facts to help you to deliver the lesson. The material is cross-referenced to the unit, or cluster of units, to which it applies.

The QCA document *3C Materials and its properties* is the backbone of this book. The structure and contents have been carefully followed. However, as the children's knowledge of materials develops so we introduce other units on the sustainable management of materials at suitable points. The background section moves back and forth between these linked themes.

Where appropriate ideas have been included for other activities to help reinforce and develop the children's understanding.

We suggest you read the whole background section before you start the programme and then reread the appropriate section before each lesson.

Appropriate vocabulary?
During the process of devising the activities, careful consideration was given to the most appropriate vocabulary. Simple phrases have been substituted for a few terms that primary aged children may rarely use, i.e. 'Out of the ground' for 'minerals', 'grown again and again' for 'renewable' and, 'will be used up' for 'finite'.

You know the abilities of the children you're working with. You can decide whether introducing the terms minerals, renewable and finite is appropriate. If you do, you could reinforce the children's understanding of the terms by playing a version of the 'I spy game' used in Unit 2, e.g. I spy on the art cupboard something made of a renewable material.

Ethical issues and children
When dealing with ethical issues and children it's very easy to present material that sounds critical of the children's lifestyles. We try to avoid such material. The attitudes and behaviour that children bring into the classroom have been acquired from other caring adults and places. If children behave in a wasteful, profligate way it's hardly their fault.

This programme supplies information that might encourage the children to change that behaviour.

Sequence of units
The units should be completed in order although you may want to develop and modify the worksheets to meet the particular needs of your children!

Development of material conservation and waste management strategies
The whole issue of conservation of material resources and waste management is rapidly evolving.

To help keep your work up to date you may want to contact some of the organisations listed in the 'Where to get additional help' section of the book.

Background information

Rats!

Rats are rodents, a species of mammal with a particular configuration of teeth. They have teeth in their cheeks and a single pair of incisors in the middle of both their lower and upper jaws. These incisor teeth continually grow throughout the creature's life to compensate for the continual process of being worn down by gnawing. The creatures are omnivores and are quite at home alongside humans. They happily feed on some of our discarded waste and are one of the creatures that convert waste to compost. However, they can damage crops in farmland areas as they hunt for cereals, vegetables and worms.

In the UK there are two main species of rat. The most numerous is the Common or Brown Rat. This species is often found beside water (e.g. streams, ditches and sewers). Four of its senses, touch, taste, smell and hearing, are excellent. In contrast the creature has poor eyesight but is talented at both swimming and burrowing.

The reproductive potential of the species is substantial! Females are sexually mature at about two months old. After a pregnancy lasting about three weeks they produce a litter of between six and eleven young. They are capable of repeating the feat five times a year!

Apart from humans the creature has plenty of enemies and these control the population. The British Mammal Society believes that the mantra 'you're never more than a few feet from a rat' is a myth. They are less numerous than most people think.

The Black or Ship Rat is not as common as its brown relative. Smaller in size, this creature is a good climber and can jump over a metre in height. It uses pipes, beams, cables and roofs as its thoroughfare between habitats. Its senses and reproductive capacity are similar to the brown rat. However its population is falling, probably due to competition from its larger relative.

Rats and disease

Rats have been historically linked with the spread of disease. The Black Death or Plague was probably spread by fleas which were parasites on the rat population of the Middle Ages. Today there are other problems.

Leptospira or Weil's Disease

Leptospira or Weil's Disease is a potentially fatal condition that can be caught from indirect association with rat's urine. Rats, with this bacterial infection, can contaminate the water, food and wet areas they travel through. Humans can catch the infection if they eat infected food, or, cuts and abrasions are in contact with infected sources. Sensible hygiene precautions obviously eliminate most of the risks.

The Weil's Disease Information Centre (address in 'Where to get additional help') believes that the following families are most at risk from the infection. Those who:

- Live in farming areas;
- Live close to inland waterways;
- Take part in water related activities such as canoeing, sailing or caving;
- Live in urban areas with a known history of rodent infestation.

The early symptoms of the disease are similar to a common cold or influenza. Later symptoms include bruising of the skin, sore eyes, nosebleeds and jaundice. The disease is curable if it's diagnosed and treated early in its development.

You obviously don't want to create a climate of fear in school but you should make it clear that children should avoid any places where rats live or visit. They should never eat or drink anything that they know or suspect a rat has been close to.

Rats are 'useful' to humans too!

Some of the children you teach may have a different experience of rats. They may keep them as clean, intelligent pets.

You might explain to the children that rats and other animals are often bred and kept in cages and used instead of humans to test the safety of new medicines and treatments. The animals are deliberately infected with a disease or injured in some way in order to test the effectiveness of some new treatment. Clearly this introduces the issue of 'animal rights'.

Those people who support the use of rats and other animals for this purpose cite the benefit to humans of the thoroughly tested treatments.

Opponents to the use of animals in this way highlight the cruelty inflicted on the creatures to develop the treatments. They will also draw attention to the inappropriate use of the animals, e.g. rats have been used to test the safety of cosmetics and others have been trained to find and detonate land mines. Legislation has been passed to protect animal rights. There should be no research using animals if an alternative exists.

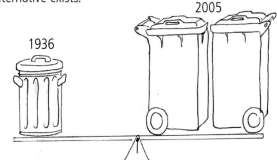

The average weekly weight of waste thrown away by each family in the UK has not changed since 1936. Then, the bins were full of ash from fires. Comparatively, the volume of waste thrown away in recent years has more than doubled.

Background information

Unit 1: Materials we throw away

QCA Science Unit: 3C

Unit 2: Survey of materials used in the classroom

QCA Science Unit: 3C

In order to help children understand about materials and how to use them wisely, this programme initially presents a set of sequential ideas. These are:

- How to identify different materials and their properties;
- The materials that we use often look very different from their source;
- Some materials come from finite sources and need conserving;
- Other materials are renewable and can be grown again and again.

Once children have acquired this knowledge they can begin to consider the consumption and disposal of materials in appropriate ways.

These units introduce the first two of these ideas. The other ideas are introduced in the following units.

Unit 3: Where do materials come from?

PSHE Citizenship 2J
Geography 2C, 5A and B

Unit 4: A materials database

QCA Science Unit: 3C ICT 1B

Many of the materials we currently use are finite and will be effectively exhausted at some unknown date in the future. It makes sense for children, in a simple way, to know the origins of the materials they use and then to sort out those which are finite from those which are renewable.

The finite raw materials are minerals from out of the ground, i.e. metals, most plastics, bricks, stone and cement and, importantly, fossil fuels (coal, crude oil, natural gas).

Renewable raw materials are those which are grown and derived from animals and plants. They include paper, wood, a few plastics and fabrics such as cotton, wool and hemp.

Of course at a more sophisticated level most of the products made from renewable materials have finite materials embodied in their manufacture. For example it is quite likely that a great deal of fossil fuel is used converting wood into paper. Then, if waste paper is recycled, more finite fossil fuel is consumed in that process too.

The origin of the common materials used in classrooms

FINITE MATERIALS

1. Metal. From out of the ground

Most metals are mined from mineral ores, i.e. they come from 'out of the ground'. Some of these ores are common and are distributed widely around the planet (e.g. iron). Others, such as gold and silver, are much rarer. Some people predict that the known reserves of some of these ores (e.g. zinc, lead, copper) may be exhausted within the children's lifetime. Other people are less cautious and believe that there are sufficient reserves to last for the foreseeable future. Whichever is true, all of the common mineral ores are mined at great environmental cost. Any new reserves that are found are likely to be in less accessible places than current reserves. Places such as Antarctica and the ocean floors may need to be exploited.

The potential for severe environmental damage will be immense.

The current mining process already impinges on valuable environments. For example, iron ore is mined in Brazil. There railways and roads, to carry the ore, have cut swathes through vast areas of rain forest. In other areas the legacy of mineral mining is water pollution. In parts of Northern Spain, arsenic, left in bygone mineral workings, has been washed out of them by rainwater. There is severe long-term damage to the surrounding environment.

In addition, huge amounts of fossil fuel energy are used to convert mineral ores to a useful end product. The carbon dioxide pollution from this embodied energy is contributing to climate change.

Climate change, global warming and greenhouse gases

For more than a century humans have been burning materials in power stations, vehicles and buildings without much thought for the consequences.

One of the by-products of burning materials is carbon dioxide gas which is released by chimneys and exhausts into the air. Although carbon dioxide is absorbed by plants during the photosynthesis process there has been a measurable increase in the gas in the atmosphere during the last century.

Carbon dioxide is one of the set of greenhouse gases which accumulate naturally in the earth's

~~~~~~~~~~~~~~~~~~~~~~~~~~~~~~~~~~

~~~~~~~~~~~~~~~~~~~~~~~~~~~~~~~~

atmosphere and are essential to life on the planet. The three main greenhouse gases are carbon dioxide, methane and nitrous oxide.

How greenhouse gases work

Much of the sun's energy that hits the planet is reflected back into space. Greenhouse gases trap some of this heat and reflect it back to warm the earth. Without these gases, life on earth would not exist. However, as the amount of greenhouse gases in the atmosphere increases, so the amount of solar energy being 'trapped' in the earth's atmosphere also increases.
Global warming and climate change are the predicted consequences of this atmospheric change.

Global warming and climate change

Over the last century there is evidence of both retreating polar ice caps and a slow rise in sea level. In addition the highest recorded average annual temperatures have occurred in recent years. These are believed to be symptoms of climate change. The predicted consequences of these changes are flooding of low-lying areas, more regular occurrence of extremes of weather (storms, droughts etc.) and changes to eco systems that will cause problems for both agriculture and wildlife.
Taking action to reduce the amount of greenhouse gases released into the atmosphere makes good sense.

2. Glass. Mainly from out of the ground

Children at school are going to be familiar with glass windows, bottles, jars and drinking glasses. These items are made from a product known as soda-lime glass.

The main ingredient is sand. If heated to 1700° Celsius the silica in sand would fuse to produce a glassy substance. However, by adding 'soda ash' (sodium carbonate) to the sand, the fusion process takes place at much lower temperatures. The main ingredient in soda ash is salt. This common chemical can be extracted from reserves in the ground or from sea water. Small amounts of other chemicals are added to the glass mixture to produce different colours.

Although there are vast reserves of silica on the planet, a great deal of energy is consumed in producing glass from raw materials. Making glass from cullet, tiny pieces of broken recycled glass, is more energy efficient.

Although recycled glass from bottle banks is often now the main ingredient in soda-lime glass the materials originally came from out of the ground!

3. Bricks and cement. From out of the ground

Bricks are made from clay. The clay is moulded, dried and then fired in an oven. The colour of the brick depends on the mineral content of the original clay.

Cement is made from either limestone or chalk. Both are rocks that were originally formed from coral or shell material that accumulated in ancient warm seas. The rock is mined and then heated to about 1450° Celsius. The material is cooled, mixed with small amounts of other minerals, powdered and packed in waterproof bags. Builders mix the cement powder with sand and water and use it as an adhesive to hold bricks or stone together.

There are large reserves of both clay and limestone. However, both the brick and cement-making process are energy intensive and release vast quantities of carbon dioxide gas into the atmosphere. The industry is a major contributor to climate change.

4. Plastic. Mostly from out of the ground

Although children will have already used vast amounts of plastic in their lives, most will be unaware of where it comes from.

Plastic is mainly derived from crude oil which is pumped from beneath the ground. Apart from pictures of a sticky black treacly substance polluting beaches most children (and adults) will have no real experience of crude oil.

Most scientists accept that crude oil is a finite fossil fuel that was formed in warm seas millions of years ago. Plants and small creatures, called plankton, thrived in the sea. When they died their remains sank to the ocean floor where they were covered by silt and sand. Over millions of years the pressure from accumulations of further silt and sand, plus heat from the earth's core, has changed the remains of these organisms into crude oil.

After hearing this information children may rightly argue that plastic is indirectly derived from plants and animals. However, unlike renewable materials, reserves of this fossil fuel are almost certainly finite.

Crude oil is obtained by drilling oil wells and pumping the substance to the surface. Then, by heating, different useful substances are separated from it. Young children will recognise several of these other products, i.e. petrol, diesel, and 'natural gas'. They may be surprised that most plastics, some fabrics, chemicals, paints and polishes are derived from crude oil too.

Equivalents to many of these products could be produced from other renewable resources. For example, in the USA some plastics are made from maize. However the crude oil based products are 'cheaper' to produce!

The reason is simple. The constituents of crude oil that are in greatest demand are petrol and diesel. When these products are produced, by-products, such as ethylene and propane are 'left over'. Converting them into plastics such as polyethylene (using ethylene) and polypropylene (using propane) makes economic sense.

Some people predict that the world's reserves of crude oil will be exhausted within 70 to 100 years. However, as with other minerals, if new reserves of crude oil are found and exploited they will almost certainly be located in inaccessible wilderness areas. Exploitation will be at an environmental cost.

Other explanations on the origins of crude oil

Some scientists believe that crude oil derives from chemical deposits trapped beneath the surface of the earth when the planet was formed. They believe that these deposits are slowly seeping up into the surface of the earth and are in a sense replacing what has already been used. If true, this theory would mean humanity could carry on consuming fossil fuels but increase still further the gases that cause climate change.

RENEWABLE MATERIALS

1. Wood and paper. From trees and other plants
The link between wooden products and trees is obvious to most children. However some children will not be aware of the link between trees and paper.

Hopefully most of the wood products used in the school will be derived from sustainable forestry. Forestry is described as sustainable when:
- New trees are planted to replace those cut down;
- The soil is protected from erosion and nutrient depletion;
- Jobs, food and materials are provided for the local population.

Many of the forests in the Developed World comply with these definitions. However, there is an environmental cost even in 'sustainable forestry'. Quite often a single species of tree is planted over huge areas of forest and this has a negative impact on local wildlife. Only a limited range of plant and animal species will be supported by this monoculture. Some species that previously existed in 'more natural' mixed forests will be threatened with localised extinction.

Wood-based products used in school, such as paper, cardboard, fibreboard and plywood, will almost certainly be

sourced from sustainable softwood forests in the Northern Hemisphere. (Sweden, Canada, Latvia etc.)

Some of the more durable items purchased by schools may contain temperate hardwoods such as oak, beech and ash. These will also probably have been harvested from sustainable European forests.

The main problem for schools is in buying products made from hardwood grown in tropical areas. Timbers such as teak, mahogany, iroko, edinam, afromosia, sapele and lauan are often harvested from unsustainable forestry. In order to obtain these few valuable species, large areas of mixed tropical forest are felled. For example, it has been estimated that only 12 of the 680 indigenous species of tree in Indonesia are harvested. If replanting does occur then only the few valuable species are replaced. This has the same impact on wildlife as mentioned above.

In addition, mahogany trees take more than 90 years to mature and iroko 150 years. Other species have a longer life cycle so there is no real incentive for logging companies to replant them. It is estimated that at least 140,000 sq. km. of tropical forest are felled and not replaced every year.

2. Straw. From trees and other plants
We have included straw on this list of materials because young children are likely to be familiar with it and it is fairly obviously grown from plants. As a renewable by-product of cereal production it has many environmental advantages over other materials. Apart from its use as guinea pig bedding, experiments at The Centre for Alternative Technology show that it is relatively easy to construct well insulated, and inexpensive buildings using straw. Properly protected, the buildings can last a lifetime. When eventually the buildings are demolished the remaining straw can be composted!

However, straw is often the by-product of cereal mono-culture with the consequential environmental effects on local wildlife and plant species.

MATERIAL THAT CAN BE EITHER FINITE OR RENEWABLE
1. Fabric
This is the last element on the worksheet and might provoke some interesting discussion and amazement among the children. We all wear bits of material that come from animals, trees and other plants, and, out of the ground!

However, if the children look closely at the origins of their clothing, every item directly or indirectly originates from animals and plants.

'Man-made fibres' (polypropylene, polyester, nylon, etc.) are derived from crude oil. Many of these synthetic textiles have particular trademarks, e.g. Terylene, Lycra etc. The environmental problems with materials derived from crude oil have been described in 'plastics' above.

The source and names of some common renewable fabrics are:
- Animals: wool, leather, silk, angora etc.;
- Trees and other plants: cotton, linen and hemp are derived from plants. Rayon is a 'man-made fibre' using modified wood pulp obtained from spruce or eucalyptus trees.

As in sustainable forestry (above) all these materials are often grown as part of a monoculture. Cotton for example is grown in huge areas in Southern USA and Egypt. Large amounts of pesticide and fertiliser, usually derived from crude oil, are added in order to sustain the crops. These chemicals destroy large numbers of the few plant and animal species that survive in the cotton fields.

Unit 5: Rat news: we know where their rubbish goes!

English 2 Reading 3, 5 & 9.
Literacy Year 4 Reading Comprehension, Non-fiction

The next two units explain the common processes of disposing of waste, i.e. landfill and incineration.

Compared to some of our European neighbours the UK has dumped large amounts of waste in landfill sites. Geologically the UK has a wide diversity of rock types in a relatively small area. Throughout the country there has been the opportunity to exploit a range of natural resources, e.g. chalk in Kent; clay in Bedfordshire, limestone in Derbyshire, slate in North Wales, coal in Yorkshire etc. Simply, wherever natural resources have been quarried or mined there is a hole in the ground! The owners of these sites have wanted to make full use of their 'economic potential' and many have been systematically filled with rubbish. 'Where there's muck there's brass (money)!' is clearly true with landfill sites.

The children you teach have inherited a culture where throwing away vast amounts of rubbish has been easy and relatively cheap. However there are several problems to be considered.

Landfill sites are running out!

There is a limit to the amount of resources that can be mined and quarried. Our throw away culture has filled many of the existing holes in the ground. In some areas, waste has had to travel many miles in order to be dumped. For example, in 2003 Bristol was sending the city waste by train to discarded brick-making clay quarries in Bedford and Northampton. Strangely, some of London's waste was being transported in the opposite direction to Cheltenham (see later).

Some waste products are toxic

Some of the objects that we use in our daily lives are potentially toxic. Batteries for example may contain mercury or cadmium. When these batteries are thrown away into holes in the ground the poisonous metals they contain have the potential to leach into the surrounding geological formations and pollute underground water supplies.

Other discarded items can contain hazardous wastes that can pollute the air around the landfill site. Products containing asbestos fibres are particularly dangerous and are known to cause cancer in those unfortunate enough to be exposed to them.

There are now strict environmental controls on the use of areas as landfill sites. They have to be lined with a waterproof material to prevent hazardous waste leaching out of the site. Clay is commonly used for this purpose.

Layers of waste are compacted and covered with soil to prevent airborne pollution and discourage vermin.

Hazardous household waste

There are many products that contain hazardous material which should be disposed of separately from other wastes. The list includes motor oils and filters, paints, varnishes, lacquer, ink, adhesives, resins, cleaning solvents, photo chemicals, medicines, pesticides, batteries, fluorescent tubes, aerosols, asbestos, bleach, printed circuit boards and computer equipment containing internal rechargeable batteries.
Each of the products should be marked with symbols which advise the user:
- Not to dispose of the item with other household waste;
- To recycle the product where possible.

A few of the listed items are used in school. Your local authority should be able to provide information about how the items can be safely disposed.

What happens to the waste in the landfill site

Most of the waste that originates from materials that come out of the ground does not change significantly once it's dumped in the landfill site. In the USA black plastic garbage bags full of waste, dumped decades ago have been unearthed. Much of the waste was in 'pristine state' and has hardly deteriorated. The evidence is that long after we've lived our lives and we have decomposed, our waste will remain. The crisp packet and the supermarket shopping bag that are discarded so frivolously are more enduring than we are!

In contrast, the organic waste that is derived from products made from animals, trees and other plants decomposes more rapidly than waste produced from other materials derived from out of the ground. This decomposition of this organic material produces a potentially more serious problem.

Methane!

In order to get as much waste as possible into the landfill sites the rubbish is compacted. There is no point in burying air! In addition, the impermeable barrier around the site prevents liquids from draining out. Landfill sites are in fact poorly managed compost heaps! They are a damp, compact, airless mass. If air is not freely available in the decomposition process of organic materials then methane gas is produced.

In some landfill sites the methane produced is collected and burned. It is either 'flared off' and its heating potential is wasted, or it is used as a fuel to heat buildings, water etc.

In other landfill sites the gas escapes into the atmosphere.

Does it matter?

Burning methane gas from landfill sites adds more carbon dioxide to the atmosphere and contributes to climate change (see above).

However there is a twist in the tale! If methane gas is not burned it causes a bigger problem. Methane is a much more potent greenhouse gas than carbon dioxide. If greater proportions of this gas are added to the earth's atmosphere then global warming will accelerate.

Unit 6: Burning rubbish in incinerators

English 2 Reading 3, 5 & 9.
Literacy Year 4 Reading Comprehension, Non-fiction

It became clear to some municipal authorities several decades ago that alternatives to dumping waste in landfill sites were needed. Many of the materials that we throw away, particularly those derived from plants and crude oil (paper, cardboard, wood, plastics etc.) are easily combustible. Some authorities recognised the potential heat energy that was 'stored' in the waste and began building incinerators to burn their rubbish.

How do waste incinerators work?

The combined technologies involved in burning waste, minimising pollution, plus generating and distributing heat and electricity are expensive. To recover the costs the incinerator needs a consistent supply of waste for the life span of the plant. An incinerator in South East London, for example, burns 420,000 tons of waste a year. There is no need for the local community to recycle any waste!

Usually a few days supply of waste is stored at the incinerator plant. This is fed into the incinerator furnace and burnt at a high temperature. The flue gas is fed through a variety of cleaning environments designed to remove pollutants. The gas is then blown into the atmosphere by a large fan.

Ash is taken out of the incinerator. This contains unburned metal waste which can be removed and recycled. The remaining ash is taken away to a landfill site. There have been some experiments to use this ash waste as a sub surface material in road building.

What happens to the heat?

Proponents of waste incineration assert that three tonnes of waste material contains as much heat potential as a ton of coal. The heat from the incinerators can be used to produce steam at high pressure that drives electricity generating turbines. The South East London incinerator produces enough electricity to power 35,000 homes.

After generating electricity the steam can be condensed and the hot water used to heat local homes and businesses.

Too good to be true?

In many ways, the incineration of urban waste seems an ideal solution to an increasing problem.

Incineration can:

* Significantly reduce the amount of waste going to landfill;
* Reduce the amount of methane produced by landfill;
* Recover some useful energy from the waste and produce electricity and heat.

However, as with all technological 'solutions', there are costs as well as benefits.

No incentive to reduce waste?

In most situations at least 65% of our current waste could sensibly be recycled. We could reduce the habitat destruction caused by exploiting virgin materials and leave finite material assets in the ground for future generations if we didn't allow our rubbish to go up in smoke.

Landfill still needed

Although incineration reduces the volume of waste going to landfill, up to 30% of the waste by weight can end up as ash. (This figure can be reduced if the waste is screened prior to incineration and materials such as glass removed.)

Some of the ash, particularly that collected by the cleaning systems in the incinerator flue, can contain high levels of toxic substances such as lead and cadmium. This hazardous waste must be disposed carefully. Friends of the Earth reported that flue ash waste from the South East London incinerator was taken by train to a landfill site in Cheltenham for special disposal.

Unseen damage from dusts and gases

Opponents of waste incineration also point to other, more sinister, implications. They focus on the emissions from the flue of the incinerator of compounds such as soot, dioxin and heavy metals.

Soot

Opponents argue that the human body has evolved defence mechanisms to prevent damage from dust in the air, i.e. the hairs in the nose are an effective filter system to prevent dust entering the lungs. However, although incinerators filter out many of the larger dust particles very tiny 'particulates' of soot escape from the chimney flues. These tiny particles elude the body defence mechanisms and can exacerbate respiratory disorders. They may also increase the risk of lung cancer.

Dioxin

Dioxin is the name given to a group of compounds. Each compound is a mixture of hydrogen, carbon and chlorine. In terms of relevancy to this project, dioxins are likely to be produced when waste containing materials such as PVC, plastics or preservative treated timber are burned. They may also be formed if recycled paper is bleached with chlorine.

Dioxin is linked with several problems. Firstly it is a very persistent chemical and does not easily break down into either its elements or other compounds. It seems to accumulate in an environment and may enter the human body in the air we breathe or in the food we eat.

Secondly, dioxin is toxic to humans. Cancer, chloracne, diabetes and hormone disruption may all be caused or exacerbated by the compound.

Heavy metals

Many products that we use and then discard contain small amounts of metals such as cadmium, chromium, lead, mercury and nickel. The metals will survive the incineration process and be discharged in either the ash or as particulates via the chimney flue. Although only small amounts of these heavy metals will be discharged into the environment the people living near the incinerator will be constantly exposed to them. There may be consequences for their health.

One effect of heavy metals in the atmosphere

Some older teachers will remember that during the 1990s infant children, living near motorways and other busy roads, were believed to be particularly vulnerable to exhaust emissions from vehicles fuelled by 'leaded' petrol. The atmospheric pollution from burning the fuel was believed to impair young children's intellectual development. 'Unleaded' petrol was introduced and motorists were given a financial incentive to use it.

A couple of decades later, most people accept the need for unleaded fuels.

Where should waste incinerators be built?

When landfill sites are full and waste keeps accumulating, incineration seems an obvious practical solution. There are obvious health problems for a community in allowing large amounts of waste to fester!

However waste incinerators are like motorways. It seems to make sense to build them until somebody decides to build one near you. In recent decades incinerators have been sited in areas of low economic value well away from the areas with the affluence that creates much of the waste.

Britain has a relatively large population in a small area. Wherever waste incinerators are built they are not far from someone's home. People will argue that if it doesn't make sense to expose young children to the lead in vehicle exhausts it doesn't seem sensible to expose them to the lead, soot or dioxins in the exhausts of incinerators either.

The bigger picture

Lots of research and development is taking place to improve the performance of waste incinerators. Problems such as those of particulates, dioxins and heavy metals may be reduced or eliminated. However large quantities of carbon dioxide will still be added to the atmosphere. Incinerators will be adding to the greenhouse gases.

Neither incineration nor landfill is likely to resolve the problem of waste. Many environmental organisations assert that technological solutions are not the answer. They claim that the only way to reduce waste is to avoid making it in the first place!

Background information

Unit 7: Why did they use that material?

QCA Science Unit: 3C

Unit 8: What happens to litter?

QCA Science Unit: 3C Geography 2C 5A & B

The National Curriculum encourages children to focus on the important properties of materials selected in the design of objects. The purpose for which the object is being used is clearly the most important criteria in its design. However, regulatory authorities are insisting that many objects are designed so that at the end of their use they have a smaller environmental impact and don't go into either landfill or incineration, e.g. the EU has developed policies for both cars and computers so component parts can be reclaimed and recycled.

If children are to become more environmentally sensitive they need to look at some of the properties of materials that affect the ultimate disposal of the object.

One of the properties of some of the materials we use is that they rot or biodegrade. All items of animal or plant origin, organic material, will all eventually decompose. To children and perhaps some adults the process of biodegrading is a bit like magic. The piece of newspaper lying in a corner of the backyard eventually just 'rots', and disappears!

Biodegrading

There are many biodegrading organisms. These eat and ingest organic material and convert it into food for plants. Children will be familiar with many of the larger biodegrading creatures such as worms, slugs and snails. Other slow moving creatures (e.g. millipedes and woodlice) perform the same task. In addition there are countless other micro-organisms that exist in the air and soil, such as fungi and bacteria, which happily decompose much of our waste. All these creatures are natural recyclers and perform the valuable task of converting organic waste to valuable plant nutrients.

How quickly does litter biodegrade?

One untidy method of disposing of waste materials is to leave them lying around as litter. Objects made of finite materials such as glass bottles, metal cans and plastic crisp packets don't biodegrade. They hang about in the environment for many years and can look ugly and create hazards.

Glass objects are probably the most permanent and dangerous litter so it does make sense to reuse or recycle them. Metal objects will gradually oxidise and decay. For example, steel cans rust quite quickly once the thin layer of tin plating that covers the surface of the object has oxidised or been removed by erosion. The oxidation of an aluminium can is a much slower process.

Most of the crude oil based plastics do not biodegrade. However sunlight can cause some plastic products to become brittle and 'photo degrade' over a period of years. A few specialised plastics are derived from plants, such as maize. These are purposely designed to biodegrade. These are more expensive than oil based plastics but are used by some 'ethical' organisations, e.g. The National Trust sends a magazine to its members in a plastic wrapper designed to biodegrade on a compost heap.

The first factor that influences the rate of decomposition of biodegradable material is the density of the material. Skeleton leaves and fossils are two useful examples to show children. Obviously, the fleshy and leafy part of both objects biodegrade more quickly than those made of either woody material or bone.

To speed up the process of decomposition of woody or bony material it is often mechanically shredded. Children may have seen branches on roadside trees and hedges, which are in danger of becoming hazardous, removed and shredded. In addition, some children may have seen 'bone meal' sold in gardening shops. Breaking these dense materials into tiny pieces increases the surface area of the material and makes it easier for micro-organisms to ingest. We chew our food for the same purpose!

Like humans, the biodegrading organisms have taken energy from the parts of plants and animals they have ingested. The remains, humified organic waste, are a valuable plant food.

You could compare this process with the food humans eat. Children may be surprised to know that human wastes, urine and faeces, both eventually become valuable plant foods too.

Biodegrading organisms are most effective when they have access to warmth, air and moisture. Biodegradable litter will decompose most quickly in a damp, warm, airy environment. Litter that is entombed in a wet airless environment will be well preserved.

If you have the stomach for it (the children will have!) you could also show the children pictures of human remains exhumed from peat bogs of Cheshire ('Lindlow Man') or Denmark ('Tolland Man'). These unfortunate souls were buried more than 2200 years ago in airless, watery graves where micro-organisms could not flourish. Fleshy parts of their bodies are preserved as well as their skeleton. You can find pictures from an internet search using either of the above names.

Unit 9: How we planned our worm test

QCA Science Unit: 3C Science 2 1 2 & 5

A really good way to help children understand the biodegrading process is to keep a small wormery in the classroom. The children will be able to see both the tunnelling and the removal of biodegradable litter from the soil surface by worms. In addition, the demonstration of setting up a wormery and completing a simple scientific procedure will help children understand the process of carefully planning and conducting a scientific test. The children will devise their own tests in subsequent units.

With the children you'll need to examine the wormery on a regular basis. To start with, they will want to see what is happening every day. Since progress is often quite slow, after the initial enthusiasm has waned, show the children the wormery once a week.

You should find the biodegradable material has been removed whilst the non-biodegradable material litters the surface.

Once the wormery has served its purpose, make a big event of returning the worms, sand and compost to a natural garden environment and deal with the tiny amount of non-biodegradable litter appropriately!

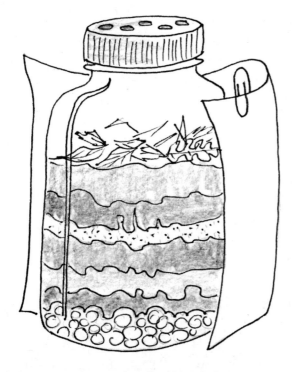

The sweet jar wormery described in Unit 9.

The physiology and life cycle of worms

These blind creatures are essential to the well-being of our planet. Colossal numbers live under soils containing organic matter. They recycle biodegradable waste, create plant foods and aerate the soil with their tunnels.

Worms have bodies made up of segments. They have no legs. They move through the soil with the help of hooked hairs which grow on each segment. These push against the soil and force the head through crevices. If the soil is compact they eat or ingest it! The digested fertile remains are left behind in their tunnels or on the surface of the earth as worm casts.

If worms are damaged when we cultivate the soil they can regenerate a few new segments. However, many damaged worms die. It is a myth that two worms are formed when the creature is accidentally cut in two.

Worms are hermaphrodite. Each worm has male and female organs. Pairs of worms mate at night on the surface of the soil by lying head to tail with their sex organs adjacent to each other. Sperm is exchanged through the skin. After mating a collar, called a 'clitellum', slides along each worm's body, collecting sperm and transferring it to the eggs. The clitellum eventually forms a cocoon of about 20 fertilised eggs which finally slips over the head and separates from the worm. The eggs hatch between one and five months later. It takes about a year for them to become sexually mature. They can live for ten years.

Unit 10: Bad news for rats

**Geography 2C 5A & B English 2 Reading 3 5 & 9.
Literacy Year 4 Reading Comprehension, Non-Faction**

One of the largest components of household waste is biodegradable material. Since landfill sites are in short supply and decomposing organic waste produces the potentially damaging methane gas, biodegradable household waste is now often being collected and treated separately. This is 'bad news for rats' as there will be less food to support their population.

This waste material is often described as 'green waste'. It is a potentially valuable material as it can be composted and reused as a soil conditioner.

Background information

Basic composting is a simple process. The waste needs a good mixture of both green leafy and woody material. It needs to be kept damp and airy. Micro-organisms ingest the waste. Like many humans, they work better when it is warmer so compost heaps decompose more quickly in summer.

Separating biodegradable waste at school

The purpose of this unit is to introduce the idea of separating different waste materials and show that it can be really useful stuff!

If your school has a garden where children can grow things then it would make sense to separate this waste in the classroom and create a school compost heap (see below). Details of using compost and growing plants in school can be found in a companion title *Learning about Life Cycles using an Organic Garden*.

If you don't have a school compost heap, the local authority or community may well have a household collection scheme for biodegradable waste and compost it centrally. It would make sense for your school to join the scheme. A bucket with a lid, in the corner of the classroom, plus a little education, are all the children need.

Community composting

Many small community composting schemes recycling 'green waste' use basic composting technology. The waste is usually piled in a sheltered rat proof silo and turned regularly by metal forks on a tractor.

To produce compost of a more consistent quality many local authorities are investing in more expensive purpose made composting machinery. Green waste is mixed and fed into the container. Often the shredded remains of hedge and tree prunings are added to the mixture. Air is forced through the biodegrading matter for two or three weeks. The partially composted material is then removed from the machine and left for a few months to 'stabilise' or 'ripen'. Providing both the site and the compost produced meet the requirements of the regulatory authorities the compost can then be sold. Once again, where there's muck there's money!

The school compost heap

You could keep a compost heap at school. Firstly decide on a sensible location for your school compost heap. It needs to be accessible on a regular basis for dumping the classroom plant waste collection. You'll also need to make sure that the pile doesn't offend neighbours or become too big a temptation for local vandals. To keep the waste in an efficient heap you can buy purpose made containers from garden centres. You could also make your own from discarded pallets fastened together with string. The shape doesn't really matter. The waste is initially going to be broken down by bacteria and fungi before worms, woodlice, millipedes, slugs etc. complete the task.

Add the plant waste, that's collected in the classroom, to the heap on a regular basis. However, if this is the only material added to the heap you'll probably produce a slimy organic mess. You need to keep air spaces open in the heap for the decomposing creatures to do their work. To achieve this, next to your plant waste collection in the classroom, keep another container for cardboard items such as 'inner tubes' of toilet rolls, egg boxes, cereal boxes etc. Get some children to help the decomposing creatures by shredding up this material during a wet playtime. Add the classroom waste and this shredded card to the compost heap in equal measures. The shredded card keeps airways open in the heap and absorbs some of the moisture from the plant waste. The decomposing creatures will ingest both kinds of waste. They need roughage in their diet just like us! As the creatures get to work the heap will warm up!

Your compost heap may also benefit from grass clippings from lawns or vegetable waste from the school kitchen. Make sure that these additions are not contaminated with herbicides etc. and that they are well mixed with equal volumes of woodier material such as the straw from the school guinea pig cage or more shredded card.

'Homemade' compost containers should be covered with a piece of old carpet etc. This prevents the waste from becoming too wet when it rains and helps keep the pile warm.

The mixture will rot down really well and eventually at the bottom of the heap you'll be left with a brown crumbly mass that can be dug out and added to the soil in the school gardens.

Unit 11: Testing materials

QCA Science Unit: 3C

Testing with less waste!

Having worked through the careful process of designing a wormery to test that worms eat biodegradable material the children are now going to design their own careful test.

In a subsequent unit children will be shown how to make their own recycled paper. So, to make a more cohesive link children are asked to devise some tests to assess the properties of different kinds of paper. At the end of the tests there will probably be a pile of used and discarded paper waste. This can all be recycled in the subsequent unit and waste minimisation put into practice.

Ideas for testing paper

(With each suggestion there is a 'discussing fairness' section which illustrates some of the points that need stressing in the plenary session.)

1. Which is the best paper to write or draw on?

Some papers are not easy to write or draw on. Children could collect samples of paper and write on them using either a pencil, felt tip pen etc. The children could assess the clarity of the image they produced or the ease that the writing instrument passed over the surface.
Discussing fairness: children will need to attempt to mark each paper sample in the same way with the same implement. There may be some problems with legibility if different coloured papers are used, i.e. black lines don't show up very well on black paper.

2. Which papers don't tear easily and could be used for packaging?

The children could use different samples of paper and attempt to tear the same shape out of the sample. Another child could count at a steady speed as an indicator of how long the tearing process took.
Discussing fairness: the same child will need to tear each paper sample and the counting will need to be consistent. Of course a child's performance in tearing may improve with practice.

3. Which paper is best for protecting presents?

The children could wrap different samples of paper around a solid object and then rub them on a hard abrasive surface whilst another child counts steadily to a predetermined number. The children could assess the damage to the surface of the paper. Discussing fairness: the pressure and vigour of the rubbing needs to be consistent, as does the abrasive surface and the 'timing'.

4. Which paper is best for a shadow puppet show?

The children could hold an object behind different samples of paper. The children could hold the paper and object up to a bright light and assess the quality of the shadow projected onto the surface of the paper viewed from the other side.
Discussing fairness: the light intensity needs to be consistent as does the way the object is held relative to the paper.

5. Which paper is best for cutting out display lettering?

Children could use scissors to cut out a letter shape from different samples of paper. The children could assess the time it took by counting or the accuracy of cutting.
Discussing fairness: the same child and same scissors ought to be used. However performance may improve with practice.

6. Which paper makes a good paper spring?

In some children's birthday cards and books there are paper 'pop up characters' fastened on a folded paper 'concertina spring'. Children could make concertina folds out of different paper samples and see which sample was the most 'springy'.
Discussing fairness: the initial paper samples need to be the same length and be folded in similar ways. A similar amount of compression needs to be applied to each spring. The term 'springy' could be evaluated.

Background information

Unit 12: Making recycled paper

Art and Design 2B, Science 3 2F

Unit 13: Which paper is best for mopping up spills?

QCA Science Unit: 3C

In the first of these units the teacher will demonstrate how to make a sheet of recycled paper. We've added this unit so that children can experience and understand the concept of recycling, i.e. reusing a material to make a similar material.

This is a messy lesson but, if you are well organised, it can be fun and memorable for both you and the children. If you've not tried to make recycled paper before, experiment for yourself at home! The instructions are in the lesson plan.

Having experienced the task yourself, you might send a note home to the children's parents or guardians, before the lesson, so the children can change into suitable clothes that can get messy. You could ask the adults to supply small amounts of natural food colouring and/or finely chopped aromatic plants (e.g. lavender, mint, onion etc.) to colour or perfume the paper.

What could you do with the recycled paper?

If children have added their own food colouring or aromatic plants to the paper they'll be able to recognise their own effort when it is dry. Some of the sheets of paper could be used in the subsequent unit that tests the absorbency of different papers. Other sheets could be used as a 'backing' material for a display (perhaps on recycled paper products),

for greetings cards or small books. At some stage you should encourage the children to recycle their recycled paper. It could be added to a community paper collection or reused in a papier mâché construction.

Whether the paper is recycled or reused make it an 'event'. Let the children see that recycling is a continuous process.

What do you do with the left over materials?

At the end of both lessons you are bound to have some remaining resources.

Pulp from making recycled paper. Don't flush the pulp down the sink or toilets. The pulp is biodegradable and is an asset if used properly. Tell the children how you are going to dispose of it. There are at least two sensible options.

- Add it to the school compost heap where it can be recycled into compost.
- Spread it around growing plants as surface mulch. The pulp will suppress weeds and be gradually dragged into the soil by worms. (You could add some pulp to the class wormery.)

Wet paper from the absorbency test. Don't just throw the wet paper away, it's still useful. It could be used in the following three ways:

1. Papier mâché masks

The children could present some of the information in this project in a presentation to other pupils. Some could wear RATS masks made from papier mâché.

2. A drying test

Ask children to devise tests on how to dry wet paper. It is very easy to modify worksheet 12 and cut and paste an alternative title, i.e. Which is the best place for drying wet paper? or Which paper is the best at drying? You'd follow the same general lesson procedures for either title. You will need a few extra resources such as string, paper clips or clothes pegs.

3. As a useful compost additive

Mixed with a green material such as grass cuttings, wet paper composts very easily.

Unit 14: Learning from the clothes bank

Mathematics 4 1 & 2

This unit uses the example of what happens to clothes deposited in a 'clothes bank' to help children understand the importance of reusing materials. The Department of

How the clothing in the clothes bank is used	Average out of ten items	% in DTI document
1 The clothes are reused and sold again as second hand clothing, often in other countries.	5	52
2 The buttons and zips cut out and the clothes cut up and reused as cleaning rags in factories.	1	12
3 The fabric is recycled and used to make the material that: fills furniture and beds; goes under carpets in homes and cars.	2	22
4 The fibres in some materials are sorted, washed and then recycled into new clothing.	1	7
5 The clothes are not good enough to reuse or recycle so they are dumped in landfill.	1	7

Trade and Industry (DTI) made an assessment in 2000 of what happened to material left in clothes banks. Their figures and the way they have been rounded and adjusted are in the table above.

Second hand clothing

Second hand clothing also includes second hand shoes (9%). Charities sort and screen the collected clothing in central venues. Garments suitable for reuse are graded. Light summer, for example, is separated from heavy winter clothing. Clothing is stored and sold at appropriate seasons. However, only about 10% of the total clothes collected in the bank are of sufficient quality to be sold in the UK. The remainder (42%) are sold abroad to 'developing countries', mainly in Africa, the Indian subcontinent and Eastern Europe. This must impact on the clothing producers in those countries.

Reused as cleaning rags in factories

Garments that are either too torn or worn can be reused as cleaning cloths. Buttons and zips are removed and the clothing is cut into squares. They are sold in various grades according to the material used (e.g. white cotton wipers or synthetics).

Recycled into new clothing and filling material

Depending on their end use, garments not fit for resale can be separated by type and by colour. Colour separation can avoid the need to re-dye. The material is shredded and pulled apart. The fibres are called 'shoddy'.

'Flocking rags' can be made from shoddy of most textile types and colour. These are sold as industrial filling materials and are used in mattresses, upholstery, carpet underlay and sound insulation panels in cars etc.

Shoddy from sorted fabrics can be combined with virgin material and spun and woven into new products.

Unit 15: Do we have to throw these materials away?

Geography 2C PSHE and citizenship 2J ICT 1B

Unit 16: Do we recycle enough?

Mathematics 4 1 & 2

Finding out what is happening in your area

Recycling is evolving at a fast rate and there are many current initiatives aimed at recycling objects as diverse as computers, mobile phones, tyres and cars. The following information is basic so that it avoids instant obsolescence and stops this book from becoming rubbish and contributing to the problem.

Background information

These units are about recycling.

Recycling is only one strategy in a waste management programme but is less important than either reducing waste or reusing waste (see Unit 14).

In addition, before you complete the final units, you will need to be sure about what are the current recycling policies of the local authority. These policies will evolve from year to year. Most councils have a Recycling Officer who will be able to tell you which materials are being recycled locally and how they are collected. There are web sites that give similar information. (See 'Where to get additional help' – page 64.)

Targets for recycling

The European Union (EU) is the major authority for implementing environmental policies and directives. Historically the UK has been poor at recycling waste compared to some of our EU neighbours. The poor performance may be due to the fact that the UK has had more landfill options (see Unit 5) than our neighbours. However policies have been implemented that will gradually bring the UK recycling rate up to that of other EU states.

Packaging waste

In classrooms and at home many of the materials wasted on a daily basis are packaging items. The EU has set targets for recycling this waste. In 2006 55% of the total packaging produced in each member state is the minimum target to be recycled. Back in 1998 six states had already exceeded that target (Austria, Belgium, Germany, Luxembourg, Netherlands and Sweden). A target of 75% has been set for such states.

Specific targets have also been set for different materials. There are good reasons for this. For example the costs and benefits of recycling glass are different from those of plastic.

UK packaging recycling targets for 2006

METALS 50%

There are two main packaging metals, i.e. steel and aluminium. Theoretically 100% of this waste could be recycled but vast amounts of tins and cans are dumped in landfill. Through a combination of education and improved recycling facilities households need to be persuaded to recycle more!

The problem of improving steel recycling is cost. Experience in the Netherlands suggests that the cost of collecting steel from homes is 2.5 times that of collection from commerce and industry.

In contrast to steel, aluminium is much more economic to recycle. Huge amounts of energy are consumed converting aluminium from its ore to a metal. The recycled metal uses much less energy. However, apart from cans, large amounts of aluminium are wasted at home, mainly as wrappings for processed foods such as cakes, pizzas and Chinese meals. Recycling this particular waste makes sense!

GLASS 60%

It is perfectly possible to recycle 100% of all glass packaging produced (bottles, jars etc.) without lowering the quality of the new glass. The main constraints to achieving 100% recycling are the costs of establishing the infrastructure ('bottle banks' etc.) and organising information campaigns. One particular problem for the UK is recycling green wine bottles. We were producing more glass for recycling than UK production could consume. Large amounts of broken glass (cullet) were exported to France at great cost! The problem has been solved by converting it to products such as fibreglass roof insulation material rather than bottles.

PLASTICS 22.5%

Plastic is difficult to recycle because production requires a very high level of ingredient purity. It is important that the different types of plastic in waste are clearly separated to achieve this purity. Most EU countries failed to achieve their meagre 2001 recycling target of 15%.

Remember, plastic is relatively cheap to produce being a by-product of the petrol and diesel fuel industry. Plastic waste has a low value and needs large volumes and a lot of sorting before it can be recycled. Schools situated in an area of high population density are more likely to have recycling facilities for plastics than those in rural or remote areas.

Sadly, most plastic packaging ends up in landfill or worse. (Some oceanographers have described the ocean floors as littered with discarded plastic waste, a material that has only been widely available for 60 years!)

EU studies suggest 28 to 38% of plastic waste could be recycled. The target has been set much lower to ensure member states achieve it!

PAPER AND CARDBOARD 60%

Unlike glass, a theoretical recycling rate of 100% is not possible for paper and cardboard products. This is because cigarette, sanitary and wallpapers cannot be recovered. In addition, composting and energy recovery through incineration can be more cost and environmentally effective in certain conditions. These are:

- Where consumption and disposal of the waste paper is some distance from paper recycling technology;
- Where expensive incineration plants have already been established;

- In countries, such as Sweden, where large amounts of virgin pulp are readily available.

During the paper recycling process the paper fibres degrade. In order to produce high grade papers as much as 40% virgin material from trees needs to be added to the pulp mix.

Do we recycle enough?

The answer to this question depends on where you're coming from.

For children from families with a tradition of recycling the relatively low target figures for UK recycling may seem a disgrace. Of course for children from families with the opposite culture the figures may seem absurdly high. The current strategy for improving the UK performance and meeting EU directives on recycling packaging waste is:

- To provide more local and doorstep recycling facilities;
- To promote education in waste reduction. The aim is for children to grow up and create a culture that accepts less profligate waste of the world's resources.

Unit 17: Less waste in our classroom

PSHE and citizenship 2A

This unit is designed to consolidate all the separate strands on why we need to reduce waste, what happens to waste, what can be recycled, reused or biodegraded into one fundamental lesson, i.e. **What can we do about waste?**

3Rs of waste management

There is a hierarchy of decisions that need to be taken in order to reduce waste. They are often called the '3Rs', reduce, reuse and recycle.

The most important decision is to reduce waste before deciding what to reuse.

Only after that option should we consider recycling, ensuring that the process of collecting and recreating the material doesn't create more environmental harm than landfill or incineration.

Previous units have explained reuse and recycling. This unit introduces the difficult concept 'Was the thing we're throwing away really needed in the first place?'

Of course it is pointless imposing your own lifestyle decisions on young children. Their lives are probably controlled by other adults. In the unit the children are asked if oranges, newspapers, sweet wrappers, milk bottles

and drinks cans are really needed. You'll need to be sensitive and help children understand that as far as consuming products is concerned there are many valid points of view. However when the children know what happens to the waste from these products it may affect their future choices.

How can we improve and organise classroom waste management?

There are seven sequential steps to reducing classroom waste:

1. Stop unnecessary waste coming into the classroom. Ask the simple question 'Do we need that stuff?'
2. Identify any items that can be reused.
3. Separate the other waste into different materials which in your locality can be recycled, biodegraded or discarded into landfill or incineration as 'absolute waste'.
4. Ensure that the waste is transferred from the classroom to the appropriate facility.
5. Monitor the 'absolute waste' destined for landfill or incineration and try to reduce it.
6. Tell everyone, pupils, teachers, caretakers, parents etc., who uses the classroom what the class are doing and why!
7. Get on and do it.

A draft set of 'Rat Rules', that you might use with your class, is included at the end of this section.

Unit 18: Which is the strongest and best egg box?

QCA Science Unit: 3C

This unit is an alternative to the last series of tasks suggested in the QCA Unit 3C *Characteristics of Materials*. QCA suggest that children carry out a test to see which pair of tights is most stretchy, making a fair comparison. The QCA project is well thought out and easy to manage. However, tights are fairly gender specific and outside the experience of most 7 and 8 year old boys. In addition there are only a limited range of reuse options for tights and most end up in landfill and don't biodegrade.

If you prefer to do the QCA test rather than our suggestion you could use the layout of worksheet 13 (*Which paper is best for mopping up spills?*) to structure and record the activity.

Background information

Unit 19: Less waste please?

PSHE and citizenship 2A

Unit 20: Sorting out the rubbish

Consolidation and assessment unit

The last two worksheets are simple activities that help bring the strands in this book together and make sense of the information.

There is some research that suggests that children between 7 and 9 years of age are the most effective group at changing family lifestyle habits. If you're careful the messages from this book will go home.

An example: Over a period of time an unusual independent school in Derby managed to persuade children and parents to become a 'no landfill school'. They provided on-site recycling facilities for paper, metal, glass and some plastic waste. Biodegradable waste from lunch boxes and the vacuum cleaner went into a compost heap and the end product was used in the school organic garden. Pupils, parents, teachers and suppliers who brought non recyclable waste to school were asked to take it away and dispose of it. The school didn't need a local authority dustbin collection and saved a large sum of money each year. It also won accolades and rewards in 'green competitions'.

The school was even rewarded by industry. Children sent the junk mail which arrived in non recyclable plastic bags back to senders. They asked the senders to put the mail in recyclable paper envelopes or take advantage of the Post Office scheme that allows junk mail to be posted without any packaging. A large catalogue supplier, who had not heard of the Post Office Scheme, adopted it, saving the cost of packaging. The school received a large cheque for the information.

Celebration. Tell others

Of course this project doesn't end when the last worksheet is completed. Encourage the children to sustain the classroom waste policy. Try to find ways to monitor and reduce the amount of 'absolute waste' going into landfill. A class assembly in front of the school will reinforce the message to older children who've heard it before. Invite the parents and governors in too. The children can be the messengers and catalyst for a less wasteful, more sustainable future.

Rat Rules!

Keep waste out of our bin.

Before you throw something in the bin ask yourself:

1. Can the object be reused?

2. Can the material be recycled?

2. Can the material be composted?

If the answer to all three questions is 'NO!' then put it in the 'Absolute Waste Bin'.

Then think, 'How can I make less waste next time?'

OBJECTIVES

- To introduce the topic.
- To review children's knowledge about materials.
- To expand the children's vocabulary in the context of materials.

MAIN IDEAS

The main object of the lesson is to stimulate children's interest in materials by using a game. Although the activity sounds simple the QCA document points out that 'Children often have difficulty in distinguishing the material from the object made from the material.' It makes good sense to spend a great deal of time in this unit practically identifying the materials used in the objects.

CLASS ACTIVITY

Resources needed
- Chalkboard/flipchart etc.
- A large cardboard box containing an assortment of about ten items that:
  - are safe to touch in controlled conditions; and,
  - could be thrown away as 'rubbish'

The items should include at least one object of each material listed in the first question. They could include: a crisp packet, plastic shopping bag, glass jam jar, wine bottle, metal drinks can, junk mail, newspaper, paper bag, broken pencil, worn out clothing etc.
- A visual aid of some of the 'words that describe materials'
- A copy of worksheet 1 for each child

Keep the lesson simple and make sure each item of rubbish is a single material. For example, separate metal screw tops from plastic bottles and show them as separate items.

Tell the children that this topic will help them learn more about both materials and rubbish. Also, the topic is introduced by a rat, which knows a lot about materials and rubbish.

Explain that there are pieces of rubbish in the box. Feel inside the box and without showing an item to the children describe how it feels. Use words that are on the visual aid. Explain the meaning of difficult terms, such as flexible or rigid, if necessary.

Ask children to guess what the item is. Give them additional clues if necessary and then show them the item. **Then ask them what material it's made of.**

Let children repeat the activity in front of the class, describing the feel of the objects. As they are removed from the box write the names of the objects on the chalkboard/flipchart. This will help the children complete question 1 on the worksheet, later in the lesson. Add interesting 'describing words' used by the children to the visual aid. **Remember, as each object is withdrawn from the box help the children identify the material used in its construction.**

Give the children a copy of the worksheet. Discuss the contents and let the children complete it.

In the plenary session help children identify materials they are 'not sure' about. Then ask questions that focus on materials, e.g. what material is the crisp packet and pop bottle made out of?

Ask some children to show the object they've drawn. Confirm the material used in its construction and listen to the words the children used to describe the object. You could add some of these words to your visual aid.

Finally share information with the children on rats, e.g. life cycle, habitat, habits, problems and benefits.

Some of the words that describe materials. Select words that are appropriate for both the materials and the children

Strong, weak, flimsy, rough, smooth, stiff, rigid, tough, firm, inflexible, flexible, stretchy, elastic, bendy, hard, soft, heavy, light, lightweight, crisp, soggy, flaky, powdery, splintery, oily, furry, brittle, laminated, layered, reinforced, rubbery, polished, moist, absorbent, sticky, grained, plaited, interwoven, permeable, waterproof, shaped, malleable, corrugated, frozen, cool, hot, tepid, chilly, wet, dry, solid, liquid, dense, loose, spongy, slippery.

Rats know a lot about materials and rubbish!

1. What material is each piece of rubbish made of?
Write the name of the rubbish in the correct space in this table.

Plastic	Crisp Packet
Metal	
Glass	
Paper	
Wood	
Fabric	
Not sure	

2. Draw one of the objects that are going to be thrown away.

3. The material used to make this object is

_____

4. These words describe the material:

_____

_____

_____

_____

_____

_____

_____

_____

_____

_____

OBJECTIVE

- To identify a range of common materials and know that the same material is used to make different objects.

MAIN IDEAS

The children are going to play a game that involves looking closely at the materials used to make objects in the classroom. They will identify materials used in the construction of the objects and sort them on the worksheet. They will learn that paper and cardboard are wood products.

CLASS ACTIVITY

Resources needed
- An enlarged copy of the worksheet on a chalkboard/flipchart
- A copy of worksheet 2 for each child

Remind the children of the content of the first lesson, i.e. the children had to recognise materials by touch.

Play the version of the 'I Spy Game' described in the Background section. During the game introduce the idea that paper and card are made from wood.

Give the children a copy of the worksheet. Tell the children that they have to look carefully at the materials that have been used to make things in the classroom.

Show them how to use the worksheet.
Select an object made of one easily identifiable material and write its name in the correct space on the enlarged worksheet.

Then identify an object made of more than one material, e.g. a table with wooden top and metal legs. Write 'table top' in the wood cell and 'table legs' in the metal cell.

Identify a book and ask the children where they would put objects made of paper or cardboard. Remind the children that paper and cardboard are made from wood. Write 'book' in the wood cell.

Finally, encourage children to use the 'not sure' cell when they are uncertain about which material was used to make an object.

Give the children time to complete the activity and then discuss their answers in a plenary session.

As the children offer correct answers ask them why a particular material was chosen for that object. (N.B. You can often elicit quite thoughtful answers when you ask why other materials were not used to make an object, e.g. why are books not made of metal?)

Sadly, even in a simple activity such as this, there are a few pitfalls that adults have created for children. For example, some plastic products have been designed to mimic other materials, e.g. plastic surfaces of classroom tables often have a wood grain pattern, and, some computers, CD players and even crisp packets have shiny plastic parts that look metallic.

Reasons for choosing materials for a particular object will include:

Plastic: light, easy to clean, often colourful, waterproof and safe near electricity, can be strong and durable.

Metal: strong, often very heavy, can be shiny, used near water, but not visibly near electricity (Some children will know that there is metal in 'electric wires' and switches etc.).

Wood: can be strong, durable, quite easy to shape, sometimes heavy but not often used near water or electricity.
Paper is flexible and lightweight. Cardboard is stronger than paper.

Glass: strong, waterproof, lets light through (translucent), can be transparent, rigid, some can be easily broken.

Fabric: usually flexible, insulates, often opaque.

Differentiation
Some children could draw the objects in the correct cell.

Survey of materials used in the classroom

Look at the materials that have been used to make things in the classroom.

Write the names of things made out of these materials.

Plastic	
Metal	
Wood	
Glass	
Fabric	
Not sure	

Unit 3 Where do materials come from?

OBJECTIVES

- To know in simple terms the origins of some common materials.
- To create and use a simple key.
- To begin to know in simple terms that some materials are finite and others are renewable.

MAIN IDEAS

The children are going to be taught how to create a set of symbols to be used as a key.

Then working with a partner or friend they are going to use their key to guess the origins of materials used in the classroom.

Finally children will be introduced to the concept of finite and renewable resources.

CLASS ACTIVITY

Resources needed

- An enlarged copy of the worksheet on a chalkboard/flipchart
- A copy of the *Highway Code* or similar resource that shows road signs
- A piece of wood, plus any other raw materials you can acquire, e.g. fleece from sheep, mineral ores, clay, sand, salt etc.
- Pencils, rubbers and coloured pencils
- A copy of worksheet 3 for each child

Using the piece of wood as a visual aid, remind the children that in Unit 2 they were told that paper was made from trees. Tell the children that, with a partner, they are going to take part in a quiz to work out where other materials come from.

Tell the children that all the materials we use come from out of the ground, animals, trees and other plants.

Using the road signs in the *Highway Code* as a visual aid remind the children that symbols are often used to give other people information.

Then, directing children to the first activity on the worksheet, ask them to suggest simple symbols that could be used to give information about where materials originally come from.

Draw some of the suggested examples on your enlarged version of the worksheet, e.g. a symbol for materials that come out of the ground could be a spade or a mechanical digger.

Direct the children's attention to the second activity on the worksheet. Tell the children it's a quiz and in pairs to make sensible guesses about where each material comes from. Show them examples of raw materials as clues. Encourage them to share acquired knowledge and then draw the appropriate symbol against each material on the worksheet.

Tell the children:

- That they may have to draw more than one symbol against some materials;
- To work in pencil so they can alter their answer at the end of the activity;
- To leave the third activity until later.

Let them complete the first and second activity.

After an appropriate time bring the children together and discuss their answers.

Metal, plastic, glass, bricks and cement and some fabrics are made from materials from out of the ground. Wood, paper, straw and some fabrics are from trees and other plants. Some fabrics (e.g. wool and leather) are from animals. Using the information in the Background section enlarge or correct children's answers. Encourage them to change the symbols on their worksheet as necessary.

Finally ask the children which of the materials will sometime in the future:

- Be easy to replace (wood, paper, straw and some fabrics: they grow on animals and plants and can be grown again. Renewable).
- Be used up (metal, glass, bricks and cement are all finite resources).

Ask children to explain their answers.

Show the children how to complete the third activity. For example they could colour the cells containing renewable materials green and finite materials red.

Fabric will need both colours!

Avoid creating misconceptions

When children are taught that some materials come out of the ground they may believe that they exist and can be exploited anywhere, i.e. they may believe that if you dig deep enough you'll find oil! Sadly that's not true. Different materials are exploited in different places. Try and use local examples and children's experience to avoid this misconception, e.g. sand is often found on beaches but clay is quarried at the local brick works.

1. Invent some symbols to show where materials come from.

Out of the ground ▼	Trees and other plants ▼	Animals ▼

2. The quiz. Talk to your friends.
Draw your symbol to show where you think each material comes from.

Material	Comes from	Material	Comes from
metal		glass	
wood		bricks and cement	
plastic		straw	
paper		fabric	

3. Choose two different coloured pencils. Colour each material in question 2.

KEY

If the material can be grown again and again colour it ☐

If in the future the material will be used up colour it ☐

OBJECTIVES

- To recognise some of the properties of materials.
- To create a simple database.
- To recognise that some properties ascribed to materials are subjective and need testing.

MAIN IDEAS

The children are going to look at a collection of objects that are being discarded and identify the properties of the materials used in their construction.

CLASS ACTIVITY

Resources needed
- An example of each of the objects on worksheet 4 (You'll need to choose two items, that are being discarded, one made of wood, the other of fabric)
- An enlarged correct version of worksheet 3
- An enlarged version of worksheet 4
- Flipchart or chalkboard
- A copy of worksheet 4 for each child

Using an (enlarged) completed worksheet from the previous session remind children of the origins of some common materials, i.e. they come from: out of the ground; trees and other plants; animals.

Tell the children that where the material comes from is one of the things we know about materials.

Introduce the term 'transparent'. Using some of the objects on the worksheet as visual examples, ask children if the material used to make the object is transparent, e.g. is the plastic in the pop bottle transparent? Is the cardboard in the box transparent?

It's difficult, but try to make sure your questions focus the children's attention on the material rather than the object.

Then introduce the term 'flexible' and repeat the above.

Explain that transparency and flexibility are two 'properties' of a material.

Ask children to suggest other properties of a material. Elicit, then write on the chalkboard/flipchart a list of simple properties that materials can possess. You can help children extend the list of properties by asking them to suggest the opposite characteristic.

The list might include:
   heavy or light,
   hard or soft,
   weak or strong,
   transparent or **opaque**,
   flexible or **rigid**,
   waterproof or **porous**,
   shiny or dull.

The terms written in bold will probably need an explanation.

Show the children a copy or enlarged version of worksheet 4. Explain that question 1 is called a 'database'. It is a simple way of showing information.

Using a glass bottle as an example, discuss with the children which of the properties the glass possesses.

With some of the properties there will be obvious answers. The glass in bottles is transparent and is smooth. Tick the appropriate rectangles. ☑

However the glass is not flexible and the material was not grown on plants or animals. Put ☒ in the appropriate rectangles.

Ask the children if they think the glass is strong. Most children will assume that it is strong but all will know that if it is treated carelessly it will break.

Tell the children to leave a rectangle blank if they are not certain that the material has the property.

Let the children complete the worksheet.

In the plenary discuss the children's answers. Let children explain the reasons for their answers. Raising uncertainties about the properties of a material is an important part of this lesson. It will help explain the need for some sort of scientific testing in a following lesson.

Finally, remind children that these objects are often thrown away. Identify the objects that are made of materials that can be grown again and those made of materials that will be used up. Discuss whether it makes sense to throw away these finite materials.

1. Tick the properties of the material used to make these objects.

Object	Transparent	Flexible	Smooth	Strong	Grown on a plant or animal
glass bottle					
cardboard box					
plastic bottle					
newspaper					
plastic crisp bag					
paper bag					
metal foil					
metal drink can					
wooden object					
fabric					

Think about these materials: paper; glass; cardboard; wood; plastic; metal; fabric.

2. Which materials are usually flexible?

_____

_____

3. Which materials can be transparent?

_____

_____

_____

4. Which materials are not grown on plants or animals?

_____

_____

_____

OBJECTIVE

- To understand that some waste materials are discarded in landfill sites.

MAIN IDEAS

Acquire information from a simulated newspaper article.

CLASS ACTIVITY

Resources needed
- An enlarged copy of the Rat News article, see below
- A copy of worksheet 5 per child

Tell children that they are going to find out what happens, in some places, to materials that are thrown away.

Read and discuss both the Rat News and worksheet with the class. You may need to display a list of words hidden in the word search.

After completing the worksheet, in the plenary, discuss their answers. Explain the environmental problems of landfill sites.

Word search answers:

Rats and micro-organisms will eat: chips, vegetables, bananas, apples, oranges, fruit, bread, meat, pasta and pizza.

Rats and micro-organisms will not eat: pots, bottles, cans, tins, bags, wrappers and packets.

Rat News

We know where their rubbish goes!

For years we've been trying to work out what humans do with their rubbish, writes chief reporter Rob Rat. Now we've discovered their secret.

MANY humans put their rubbish in plastic sacks or bins. They leave these containers outside their homes and the rubbish is collected and taken away by a dustbin lorry. Amongst the rubbish is food that rats enjoy!

Huge holes in the ground

The rubbish is taken to huge holes in the ground called landfill sites. These holes were left after materials were dug out of the ground. The materials were used for making bricks, cement, glass or other things.

Lined with waterproof material

Before any rubbish is dumped in the landfill site, a waterproof material is spread around the side of the hole. This stops any liquids in the rubbish from draining out of the hole and polluting other areas.

Rats need to be quick

If rats want to eat some of this waste in the landfill site, they need to be quick. After layers of rubbish are tipped in the hole, humans with bulldozers push soil over it. Once the rubbish is buried it's difficult for rats to find and eat the food.

They say 'rubbish rots!'

If the food is buried it's eaten by worms and tiny creatures called micro-organisms. Most humans don't know that this rubbish is eaten; they just say, 'The rubbish rots.' Of course, glass, metals and most plastics don't rot. They're not eaten. They are just left in the hole as waste.

Find the nearest landfill site!

We think rats should go and quickly search the nearest landfill site. You might find huge amounts of delicious food waiting to be buried.

Rat News: We know where their rubbish goes!

Read Rat News. Answer these questions in sentences:

1. Where does the rubbish go to when it has left the home?

_____

_____

2. What was dug out of the holes in the ground?

_____

_____

3. Why is a waterproof material put around the side of the hole before rubbish is dumped?

_____

_____

4. Hidden in the word search are things that get dumped in landfill sites.
Colour the hidden word 'rat', then find:
- Waste foods that rats, worms and micro-organisms will eat;
- Things that don't get eaten by rats and micro-organisms.

c	h	i	p	s	p	o	t	s	v
d	r	b	a	n	a	n	a	s	e
c	a	n	s	r	a	t	p	b	g
o	f	y	t	i	n	s	p	o	e
r	r	b	a	g	s	w	l	t	t
a	u	b	r	e	a	d	e	t	a
n	i	n	m	e	a	t	s	l	b
g	t	p	i	z	z	a	s	e	l
e	d	p	a	c	k	e	t	s	e
s	l	w	r	a	p	p	e	r	s

Write the words you find in the table.	
Things that rats and micro-organisms:	
will eat	will not eat

Unit 6 Burning rubbish in incinerators

OBJECTIVES

- To know that in some places rubbish is burned to provide heat and power.
- To provide a stimulus for a movement and drama lesson.

MAIN IDEAS

To read a newspaper article on incinerators and complete a comprehension task.

CLASS ACTIVITY

Resources needed

- Enlarged copy of Rat News
- Worksheet 6 per child

Remind children of the previous lesson; explain that not all waste is dumped in landfill sites. Share the Rat News article with the children. Discuss the incineration process. Ensure understanding of the terms written in bold in the text.

Show the children how to complete the worksheet. Make sure the children understand the advantages and disadvantages of incinerating materials. In the plenary, discuss the children's answers to the worksheet.

Movement and drama

The process of waste incineration (i.e. materials discarded, collected then compressed in lorries, dumped at the incinerator, mechanically conveyed to the furnace, burnt to produce heat and power or recycled) is an excellent stimulus for creative activities, especially movement and drama.

Rat News

Disaster for Rats

AS EVERY good rat knows, one of the best places to find delicious food is to look in the waste that humans leave lying around. But now rats are facing a disaster, writes chief reporter Rob Rat. In some places, this rubbish is burnt!

Incinerators in big cities

Many big cities have almost run out of landfill sites where rubbish can be dumped. Instead, lorries collect the rubbish from people's homes and take it to a huge building. Here the lorries are emptied and the waste is carried by machine into a **furnace** where it is burnt.

Heat makes electricity

As the rubbish is burnt it heats water in a **boiler**. Steam is produced in the boiler and this is used to spin a **turbine** which makes electricity. Thousands of homes use the electricity that is made by burning rubbish.

Not everything burns

Some of the materials, that are thrown away as waste, don't burn in the furnace. Metals and glass, for example, do not burn like paper, wood and plastic.

Some materials are recycled

Materials that have not burned are collected from the furnace, sorted and then taken away. Metals and glass are taken to factories where they are recycled. The materials are used to make new things.

There is still some waste

You would think that after the burning and recycling that there would be no waste left. However there is a small amount of dirty ash left and this is taken away and dumped in landfill sites.

Keep away from incinerators

We've discovered that many humans do not like incinerators. They are worried about the smoke and ash. They think both may contain harmful dust and chemicals. We think rats should keep well away from these incinerators.

When you have read the *Rat News* answer theses questions in sentences.

1. Why is rubbish being burnt in some cities?

_____

_____

2. What is the heat from the burnt waste used for?

_____

_____

3. Which materials can be burned in the incinerator?

_____

_____

4. Which materials don't burn but can be recycled?

_____

_____

5. Some people like incinerators but others don't like them. Write what you think about incinerators on this banner.

Unit 7   Why did they use that material?

OBJECTIVE

- That materials are suitable for making a particular object because of their properties and that some properties are more important than others when deciding what to use.

MAIN IDEAS

The children will be shown a collection of objects. They will identify the material used to make each object and the properties of the material. They will consider which of those particular properties were most important in the design of the object.

CLASS ACTIVITY

Resources needed
- A display of a wide variety of objects each made of a single material, i.e. glass, metal, plastic, wood, paper, fabric
- Chalkboard/flipchart
- Two or three enlarged copies of worksheet 7 prominently displayed
- A copy of worksheet 7 for each child

Tell the children that they are going to think about some of the properties of the materials which are used to make things. Then, later in the lesson, they will use that information to play a game.

Remind the children of Unit 4 and ask them to help you make a list on the chalkboard/flipchart of some of the properties of materials. Your list might include: heavy or light, hard or soft, weak or strong, transparent or opaque, flexible or rigid, waterproof or porous, smooth or rough, and shiny or dull.

Show the children an enlarged version of the worksheet and use it to structure the next part of the lesson.

Invite children to complete different sections of an enlarged worksheet as you progress through the lesson. The class will pay close attention to the efforts of other children!

Show the children one of the objects. Get a child to draw a quick sketch of it in the correct space on the enlarged worksheet. Identify the material used to make the object. Let a child write the material in the correct space on the enlarged worksheet.

Using the list of properties compiled on the chalkboard/flipchart discuss which of the properties apply to this material. Let a child write them in the appropriate space on the enlarged worksheet.

Focus on the last question on the enlarged worksheet. Now, with the children look at all the properties that have been listed for this material. Decide from this list why the material was used to make the object.

Repeat this section of the lesson with another object on another enlarged copy of the worksheet.

Give the children their copy of the worksheet. Tell them to chose one object and complete the work.

Allow plenty of time for the plenary session. In it play a game.

Select a child to read their answers to question 4, i.e. describe why the material was chosen.

Before you ask the class to identify the child's object discuss with the class the range of materials the child could be describing. Then, ask the other children to identify which object was being described.

Finally, discuss with the children why a particular material was chosen to make the object rather than another. Particularly focus on objects made of finite materials (metal, glass, plastic etc.). Ask if the object could be made of renewable materials.

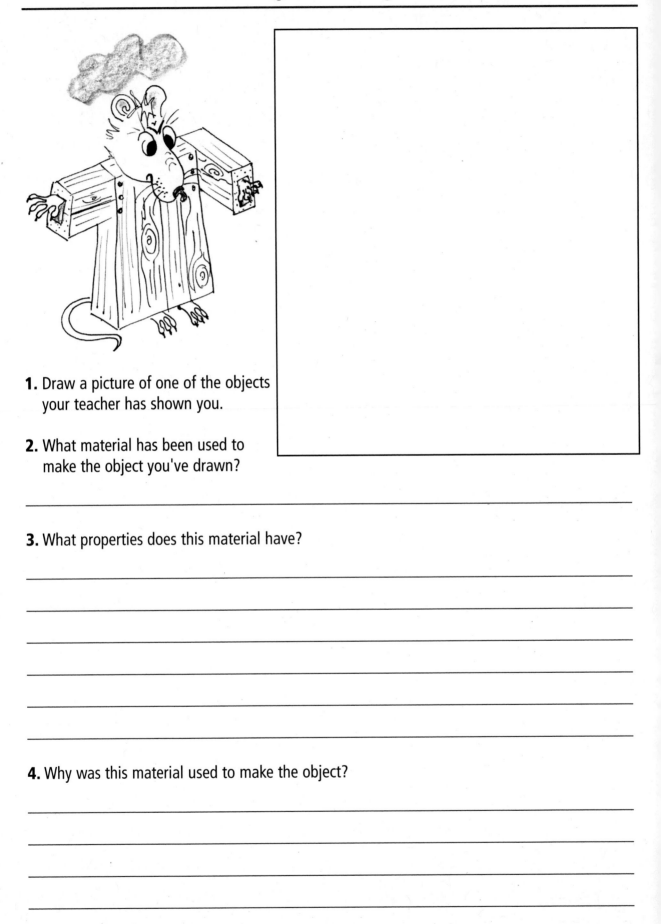

1. Draw a picture of one of the objects your teacher has shown you.

2. What material has been used to make the object you've drawn?

_____

3. What properties does this material have?

_____

_____

_____

_____

_____

_____

4. Why was this material used to make the object?

_____

_____

_____

_____

Unit 8   What happens to litter?

OBJECTIVES

- To understand that one of the properties of some materials is that they biodegrade.
- To know in simple terms that some materials biodegrade at different rates.

MAIN IDEAS

Using a key, the children will discuss and insert information on a pictorial database.

CLASS ACTIVITY

Resources needed
- An example of each of the items in the second table on the worksheet
- Some skeleton leaves, fossils and seed compost
- Enlarged copy of the worksheet
- A copy of worksheet 8 for each child

Tell the children that they are going to think about what happens to materials that are left around as litter.

Give them a copy of the worksheet and together read and discuss the paragraph at the top of the page.

The contents are simple so in the course of the discussion cover the following more detailed points:

- There are many creatures in the air and soil that 'eat' our waste;
- These creatures include worms, slugs, snails, woodlice, fungi, bacteria and a host of other micro-organisms;
- These creatures eat the materials which originated by growing on plants and animals;
- Sometimes this process is called 'rotting' but the correct term is 'biodegrade';

- That biodegradability is another property of materials;
- Some materials biodegrade quickly (e.g. paper) while others biodegrade slowly (e.g. wood);
- When materials biodegrade they don't disappear. They change, often into a food for plants in the soil;
- Litter materials that don't biodegrade can spoil the environment for many years.

Show children examples of skeleton leaves, fossils and seed compost. Elicit that leafy and fleshy parts change into plant food and biodegrade more quickly than woody or bony parts.

With the enlarged copy, show the children how to complete the key on the worksheet. Make the key fun. Use grotesque symbols (e.g. as below) to represent biodegrading organisms. Make a different facial expression on the 'creature' as the main distinguishing element of the key. This makes it easy for children to amend incorrect guesses.

Direct the children's attention to the second table. Tell the children to talk with their friends. They should think about the origins of litter materials and guess what happens to them. Let the children work through the worksheet in pencil so they can rub out and change answers.

In the plenary identify the material each item of litter is made of and what will eventually happen to it. **Ensure children understand that renewable materials biodegrade and finite materials don't.** Encourage children to amend incorrect guesses.

Worksheet 8 answers

Assuming the litter is left on the ground in a damp mild climate the answers are:

Will biodegrade and disappear in less than a year: paper bag, banana skin. Will biodegrade slowly and take several years to disappear: wooden lollipop stick, woollen glove. Will not biodegrade and can stay in the same place for many years: plastic crisp packet, nylon sock, metal drinks can, plastic shopping bag.

Example key about what happens to litter	
It biodegrades and disappears in less than a year.	
It biodegrades slowly and can take many years to disappear.	
It does not biodegrade and can stay in the same place for years.	

Many of the materials in litter are eaten by worms and tiny creatures. The materials biodegrade and change into food for plants. Other materials that are not eaten can lie in the same place for many years.

1. Draw symbols for this key.

My key about what happens to litter	
It biodegrades and disappears in less than a year.	
It biodegrades slowly and can take many years to disappear.	
It does not biodegrade and can stay in the same place for years.	

2. Write answers to say where the materials in the litter come from.
(Out of the ground, plants, animals.)
Choose a symbol from your key and guess what will happen to the litter.

Which material is the litter made from?	Where did the material come from?	What will happen to the litter?
glass bottle		
paper bag		
metal drinks can		
plastic crisp bag		
woollen glove		
nylon sock		
wooden lollipop stick		
banana skin		
plastic shopping bag		

OBJECTIVES

- To learn how to plan a safe test.
- To see that worms remove biodegradable waste from the surface of the soil.

MAIN IDEAS

The lesson shows children the planning required to:
- carry out a test;
- care for worms in the classroom.

CLASS ACTIVITY

Resources needed
- A large transparent plastic container with pre-drilled drainage and air holes (a screw top sweet jar is ideal)
- Small amounts of dried sand (two different colours if possible)
- Peat free garden compost, gravel, damp shredded card
- Some garden worms
- Black paper and elastic bands to cover the container
- A couple of litres of water
- A bowl
- Some small amounts of biodegradable material, e.g. paper, leaves, pencil shavings, straw etc.
- Some small pieces of safe non-biodegradable material, e.g. small pieces of plastic crisp packet, metal cooking foil etc.
- A copy of worksheet 9 for each child

Remind children of the previous lesson and ask them to explain the term 'biodegradable'.

Remind children that one of the creatures that removes and 'eats' biodegradable materials is the earthworm.

Tell the children that they are going to:
- Care for some worms in a wormery in the classroom;
- Plan a test to see which food the worms prefer.

Show the children the plastic container. Elicit from the children the purpose of the drainage and ventilation holes.

As you add the following layers of material into the container explain the purpose of each layer.

Gravel:
This is to enable excess water to drain away.
Alternate layers of garden compost and sand:
The compost provides food and bedding. The sand aids the worm's ingestion of food.

Stand the plastic container in the bowl and carefully water the contents of the wormery until water drains from the base.

Explain that worms need to be kept in a damp environment as they breathe through their moist skin.

Add a layer of damp shredded card to the surface of the wormery as a bedding layer.

Show the children how you will cover the outside of the wormery with sheets of black paper held with elastic bands to create a dark environment for the worms.

Now show the children the biodegradable and non-biodegradable materials you intend to put on the surface of the wormery to test the worms' food preference. Mix the materials together and spread them as a layer on top of the damp card. Explain that you have excluded some materials from the mixture (e.g. glass and sharp metals) because you want to keep the worms and the children safe.

Carefully put the garden worms into the wormery.

Finally show the children where you will keep the wormery. They need to be kept out of direct sunlight and free from incessant vibration (a warm cupboard is ideal).

Give the children a copy of the worksheet and discuss how to complete it.

In the plenary discuss the children's answers to the final question on the worksheet. Explain that:
- The worms will probably burrow into the wormery to feel safe from predators;
- That you'll uncover the sides of the wormery at regular intervals to view the worm's tunnels and see which materials they have removed from the surface and eaten.

Answer the children's questions on the life cycle and physiology of worms (see Background page 15). Tell the children that the worms will be released into a natural environment in a few weeks.

How we planned our worm test

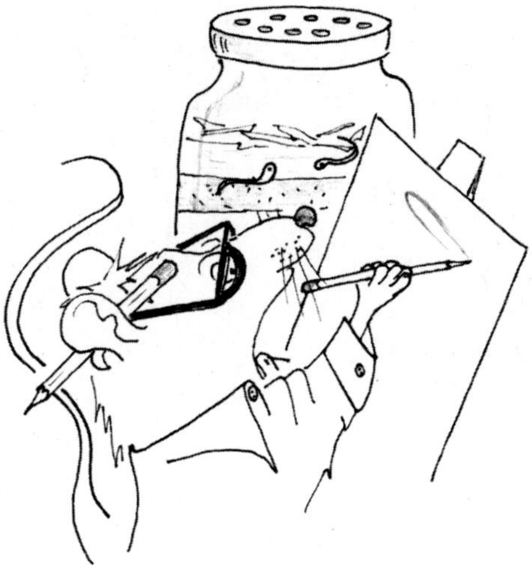

1. What are we trying to find out?

2. How are we going to look after the worms?

3. Draw a picture of the wormery. Label the different parts.

4. What do you think will happen?

OBJECTIVES

- For children to understand that biodegradable waste can be collected and composted.
- The waste is recycled into 'plant food'.

MAIN IDEAS

The children read a 'letter' from a rat complaining to another rat about a new 'green waste' collection.

The children answer comprehension questions and complete a simple crossword.

CLASS ACTIVITY

Resources needed
- Enlarged copy of the letter at the foot of this page
- A worksheet per child

Tell the children that in some parts of the country there is a kind of waste collection called 'green waste'.

Display and read with the children the enlarged letter. Use the letter as the basis of a question and answer session to ensure comprehension.

Make sure the children know how to complete the tasks on the worksheet and let them complete it.

In the plenary discuss their worksheet answers. Tell them about any local or school 'green waste' collections.

Biodegradable puzzle answers

1. Bags **2.** Sticks **3.** Flowers **4.** Card **5.** Apple **6.** Orange **7.** Grass **8.** Banana **9.** Dead **10.** Green

---

Rat News

Letters Page

MORE bad news for rats (A letter from a reader, Rita Rat). I read the articles you wrote for *Rat News* about landfill sites and incineration. They were very interesting. I thought I should tell you about another problem for rats. In our city humans have started something new. They are not dumping waste materials made from plants and animals in the landfill site. They are collecting it in bins at their homes. They call it 'green waste!'

Once a week a lorry collects the green waste and takes it to a special site. There the green waste is mixed together and kept damp. It is ventilated. Then, tiny creatures, far too small for rats to see, eat the waste!

As the waste goes through the bodies of the tiny creatures it changes into compost. Compost is a kind of plant food that humans put on their crops to help them grow! Humans are being very clever. They are recycling their biodegradable waste and feeding their crops. There won't be any waste material from plants and animals to feed us rats. There could be a big problem for rats if this 'green waste' idea is used in other cities. We could starve. I thought you should know about it.

Rob Rat replies: Rita's letter is very interesting. We shall find out more about this 'green waste' idea. We'll publish more information in a few weeks time.

1. Rob Rat made some notes from Rita's letter. What did he write?

A. What is 'green waste?'

_____

_____

_____

_____

B. What happens to 'green waste' after it is collected from people's homes?

_____

_____

C. How is 'green waste' turned into compost?

_____

_____

D. How is compost used?

_____

_____

2. Look at this puzzle. The answers all biodegrade.

  1. Tea b--- from teapots.
  2. St---- and twigs from trees.
  3. An old bunch of f------.
  4. Toilet roll tubes made of c---.
  5. A---- cores.
  6. O----- peel.
  7. G---- cuttings.
  8. B----- skins.
  9. D--- leaves in autumn.
10. This waste is sometimes called g---- waste.

			1	b			
		2		i			
		3		o			
	4			d			
5				e			
6				g			
		7		r			
	8			a			
	9			d			
1	0			e			

Unit 11 Testing materials

OBJECTIVES

- To obtain evidence to test scientific ideas.
- To plan and carry out a test safely.
- To decide whether the test was fair.

MAIN IDEAS

Children in small groups are going to devise a simple safe method of testing a property of a material. They'll plan their test, carry it out and then review the test.

CLASS ACTIVITY

Resources needed
- A wide range of different used papers, e.g. exercise, sugar, tracing, crepe, tissue, kitchen, newsprint, wrapping, etc.
- Worksheet per group
- Other class resources as appropriate for the testing

Show the children the wormery from the previous unit. Remind them that you planned and carried out a careful test to see which materials worms prefer as food. Look and discuss how the worm activity is progressing.

Tell the children that they are going to plan and carry out their own scientific tests.

Tell the children that the material they are going to test is paper.

On a flipchart/chalkboard, with the children compile a list of the properties and uses of paper. Your list will probably include:
- Paper is often: light, flexible, opaque, porous.
- It biodegrades and burns.
- It can often easily be torn or cut.
- It can be used for: writing, printing, reading or packaging.

Show the children a collection of paper products and compare the properties and performance of papers in two different circumstances, as in the following examples.

Example 1

Directing their attention to a paper towel and a piece of exercise paper, ask the children: are all these papers good for writing on?

(Most children will know that it's quite difficult to write on the paper towel.)

Having established that there is a difference; ask the children how they would test how easy it is to write on different papers. They'll probably suggest writing on different samples of paper.

Example 2

Now direct children's attention to a different property, i.e. paper can be torn.

Show the children some corrugated card and a piece of newspaper, ask: which paper is easiest to tear?

From experience the children will probably pick the newspaper.

Show the children the enlarged copy of the worksheet.

Ask the children how they would devise a test to find out which paper is easiest to tear. As you elicit cogent safe answers, complete the first two sections on the enlarged worksheet as an example for the children.

Ask the children to look at the properties and uses of paper and suggest other tests, e.g. which is the best paper to package a gift?

Which paper could be used for a shadow puppet show? (See the Background page 17.)

Let the children work in pairs and give them a copy of the worksheet. Tell them to plan their test. Monitor the children's plans.

If some children have difficulties at this stage, bring the class back together and share ideas. Encourage safety but accept naiveté. Tests which have lots of inbuilt unfairness can be sensitively used to help the discussion in the plenary session.

When the children have completed the worksheet bring the class together.

Ask groups to explain what they tested. Discuss how fair each test was, and ask children to suggest improvements.

Finally, don't waste the paper used in the lesson. Bits that are left over should be torn into tiny pieces and kept for Unit 12, Making recycled paper.

1. What are you trying to find out?

2. How are you going to do it?

3. What did you find out?

4. Was your test fair?

Unit 12 Making recycled paper

OBJECTIVES

- To experience and understand the concept of recycling.
- To know the range of paper products that can be recycled.

MAIN IDEAS

The children will be shown the process of making recycled paper. In supervised pairs they'll make some sheets of recycled paper. Each child will complete a word search on paper products that can be recycled.

CLASS ACTIVITY

Resources needed

- An old picture frame, about 30 cm x 20 cm to use as a mould; a piece of nylon curtain, agricultural fleece etc. to stretch over and pin to the mould; drawing pins; a shallow container slightly larger than the mould; pieces of cloth larger than the mould; i.e. tea towels, felt, old T-shirts etc.; potato masher; a sieve; washing up bowl and bucket; a flat object larger than the mould, e.g. wooden board or tea tray; newspaper; shredded waste paper
- Suitable clothes for a messy activity
- A copy of the worksheet for each child
- Examples of stationery, packaging, newsprint etc. that contain recycled paper
- **Additional optional:** natural food colours, aromatic plants. An additional classroom assistant

Preparation before the lesson

1. Tear up pieces of waste paper into small pieces and soak in a bucket of water overnight.
2. With drawing pins fasten the piece of agricultural fleece or net curtain tightly to the mould.
3. Before the lesson cover a flat table with newspaper. Lay a piece of cloth on top.

In the lesson

Tell the children that they are going to make some sheets of recycled paper. Demonstrate the following process:

1. Using the sieve, remove some soaked waste paper from the bucket. Rinse it and put it into the washing up bowl;

2. Just cover the sieved waste paper with water and mash it into a pulp with the potato masher. Try and get the suspension smooth. It needs to look like thick creamy milk. So add more water or waste paper if necessary;
3. Tip some of the pulp into the shallow container and at this stage add natural food colours or shredded aromatic plants to colour or scent the paper. Stir the mixture. Slide the mould into the pulp. Gently move the mould to try and capture a smooth layer. Lift the mould above the container and let some of the liquid drain back into the pulp;
4. Gently invert the mould above the cloth on the newspaper covered table;
5. Carefully remove the 'recycled paper' from the mould so that it lays flat on the cloth;
6. Cover the sheet of recycled paper with another cloth.

Supervise pairs of children in the paper making process, building up an alternating pile of cloth and recycled paper. The children should complete the word search on the worksheet when not making paper.

When all the children have had their turn.

Put the flat object onto the pile of recycled paper and clothes. Place something safe and heavy on top of the flat object to compress the pile. (A pile of books would do!)

Begin the plenary session. Discuss the answers to the worksheet and show the children some other products that are clearly made from recycled paper.

At least an hour later spread out some dry newspapers on a desk. Remove the weight and flat object. Carefully peel each sheet of damp paper away from the cloth and lay it on the newspaper to dry. Once dry the sheets of recycled paper could be ironed.

Word search answers

Things made of paper that can be recycled:
card; book; booklet; leaflet; notebook; newspaper; letter; envelope; magazine; catalogue; postcard; note; cardboard; comic; bags.

Materials, not paper, that can be recycled:
glass; metal; fabric.

Creatures that may live near rubbish:
worm; rat.

Food wrapped in paper:
chips.

c	o	m	i	c	d	f	r	b	a	g	s
a	s	d	c	a	r	d	b	o	a	r	d
t	f	a	b	r	i	c	w	o	r	m	f
a	r	a	t	d	g	j	h	k	l	z	c
l	v	n	n	e	w	s	p	a	p	e	r
o	m	a	g	a	z	i	n	e	m	b	q
g	l	a	s	s	h	l	e	t	t	e	r
u	w	r	m	n	o	t	e	b	o	o	k
e	n	v	e	l	o	p	e	c	h	i	p
t	o	y	t	p	o	s	t	c	a	r	d
u	t	o	a	l	e	a	f	l	e	t	p
s	e	d	l	g	b	o	o	k	l	e	t

Look at this word search

1. Find at least 12 things made of paper that could be recycled.

_____

_____

_____

_____

_____

_____

_____

_____

2. Find three materials, that are not paper, that can also be recycled.

_____

_____

_____

3. Find two creatures that might live near rubbish.

_____

_____

4. Find a food that was wrapped in paper.

_____

OBJECTIVES

- To plan a test to compare the absorbency of different papers.
- To decide what evidence to collect, considering what evidence to collect, what to change, and what to measure.
- To make comparisons and draw conclusions.

MAIN IDEAS

Following a class discussion, in small groups, the children will plan and carry out a test.

CLASS ACTIVITY

Resources needed

- A wide selection of used papers in different sizes. Include: some of the children's 'recycled paper' from the previous unit; some kitchen towels; some non porous papers such as grease proof paper, tracing paper; sugar paper etc.
- Water
- A variety of simple fluid measuring devices such as teaspoons, plastic measuring syringes, cups, measuring cylinders etc.
- A variety of waterproof containers, such as buckets, bowls etc.
- Scissors, rulers, pencils
- Enlarged copy of the worksheet
- A flipchart/chalk board
- A copy of the worksheet for each child

Remind and monitor the progress of the 'worm test' from Unit 9. Remind children of the tests they carried out on paper in Unit 11 and how the children decided that some of the tests could be improved.

Give each child a copy of the worksheet and use each question to structure the teaching session.

Tell the children that they are going to find out which kind of paper is best for mopping up spills.

Focus on the word **best**.

Ask the children what they think it means. (Some children will probably focus on what they think is the answer to the test. They may say kitchen towels are best.)

Direct the children carefully then elicit, and write on the flipchart/chalkboard a variety of answers, such as:

- The paper that will soak up the most water;
- The paper that will leave the surface driest;
- The paper that will soak up the spill with the least rubbing or wringing out.

Choose one of these sentences and rewrite it in the answer rectangle to question 1 of the enlarged worksheet.

Discuss with the children how they would devise a test stressing: what evidence they need to collect; what needs to change or stay the same; what to measure.

Elicit the children's help to complete question 2 on the enlarged worksheet.

Having decided on an appropriate test demonstrate it on a single sample of paper.

Show the children how you measured the result and write the result as a sample in question 3 on the enlarged worksheet.

Show the children how to complete the final question on the worksheet. Encourage them to rank the performance of the papers.

In small groups, let the children plan and carry out their test.

When the tests are complete make sure the children deposit wet waste paper in a central separate collection.

In the plenary discuss children's tests. Praise aspects of the tests that demonstrated fairness.

Discuss how the class should deal with the wet paper waste. It could be used in papier mâché art work or biodegraded in a compost heap. Don't throw it straight in the recycling box! Paper recycling organisations prefer to collect dry paper.

Which paper is best for mopping up spills?

1. What are you going to try and find out?

2. What are you going to do in your test?

3. What are your results?

4. What did you find out?

OBJECTIVES

- To know that many discarded items can be reused.
- To use keys and consolidate information into bar charts.

MAIN IDEAS

The children are given a worksheet and some verbal information about what happens to clothing deposited in a 'clothes bank'.

The children complete bar charts and then they recognise, list and discuss other reusable items.

CLASS ACTIVITY

Resources needed
- A collection of ten old items of clothing
- Coloured pencils
- Enlarged copy of the worksheet
- A worksheet per child

Remind children of previous units and ask them what we can do to stop wasting materials such as paper, e.g. *recycle the material*.

Tell children that there are other ways to stop the waste of materials, e.g. *many materials can be reused*.

Ask the children to explain the difference between recycling and reusing.
(Recycling: The **material** in the object is used again. Reusing: The **object** is used again for the same or different purpose.)

Give the children a copy of the worksheet.

Make sure children understand the term 'clothes bank'.

Explain that many thousands of clothes are put into clothes banks every year. The clothes banks are run by charities who earn money by selling the clothes or materials. The clothes are collected from the bank and sorted. The people who sort the clothes can decide which one of five ways to use the clothes.

Explain, using the old clothes as a visual aid the five possible ways (see worksheet) the clothes can be sorted. Elaborate on the basic information with additional informa-tion from the Background section. Stress the terms 'recycled' and 'reused' to make sure children understand the difference.

Now on the enlarged copy of the worksheet demonstrate how to colour in one row in the table as a key. Complete the appropriate column in the first of the two bar charts.

Point out that the terms reused, recycled and landfill are highlighted in the text and show the children how to complete question 3.

Finally, tell the children to think about and list other things, which like clothes, can be reused.

Let the children complete the worksheet.

In the plenary discuss:
- The patterns in the bar chart.
- The lists of reusable objects.

The list could include:
In the classroom: newspapers, yoghurt pots, margarine tubs. The backs of worksheets etc. have been reused for decades, but not for their prime purpose!

At home: glass milk bottles are meant to be reused for the same purpose many times to justify the energy used in making them. Ink jet cartridges can be refilled too. Rural children will know that cooking gas is often sold in reusable cylinders.

Gardens and allotments: are great places to see objects being reused for alternative purposes. Plastic bottles become mini slug proof greenhouses, wooden pallets surround compost heaps and carpets keep the compost warm. Old sheets are frost protectors and barrels from every conceiv-able industry are used as water butts.

Make sure that children understand that 'reusing' reduces waste.

OTHER ACTIVITIES

Look at some waste objects that are being thrown away. Get children to suggest and write both practical and bizarre ways to reuse the object.

UNWANTED CLOTHES

Many people give old clothes to charity. They put them in a clothes bank.

Do you know what happens to the clothes people put in the clothes bank?

1. Colour each row in the table a separate colour to make a key.

Out of every ten items that are left there:

1	The clothes are **reused** and sold again as second hand clothing, often in other countries.	5
2	The buttons and zips are cut out and the clothes cut up and **reused** as cleaning rags in factories.	1
3	The fabric is **recycled** and used to make a new material that fills furniture and beds or goes under carpets in homes and cars.	2
4	The fibres in some materials are sorted, washed and then **recycled** into make new fabric for new clothing.	1
5	The clothes are not good enough to reuse or recycle so they are dumped in **landfill**.	1

2. Use the same colours and row numbers. Make a bar chart to show what happens to clothes that get put in a clothes bank.

1	2	3	4	5

3. Look carefully at what happens to the clothing. Some is **recycled**, some is **reused** and sadly some goes into **landfill**.

Make a bar chart to show what happens to the clothes.

recycled	reused	landfill

4. On the other side of the paper, list other things that can be reused instead of being thrown away.

OBJECTIVE

- To know that materials, other than paper, can be recycled and to know where to recycle them locally.

MAIN IDEAS

Following a discussion on the materials that can be recycled locally, the children are asked to answer questions about a pictorial database. Then they design a poster to tell other children what can be recycled locally.

CLASS ACTIVITY

Resources needed
- Steel tin and aluminium drinks can, glass bottle, plastic container, newspaper, cardboard drinks carton
- Magnet
- A worksheet per child

Important: You'll also need to find out from the local authority or from collective knowledge which local recycling facilities exist.

Remind children of previous units. Revise the meaning of:
Recycled Using the material in things that are thrown away to make the same material.
Reuse Objects that can be used again for the same or different purpose. Explain that it is often better to reuse objects before they are recycled.
Biodegrade Materials that are eaten by worms and other tiny creatures; the material is recycled into plant food. Explain that biodegrading is another form of recycling. The animal and plant remains change into plant food. This helps new plants and animals to grow.

Ask the children why it is important to recycle and, from their experience, what other materials can be recycled. The list will probably include metals (drink cans and tins), glass (often separated by colour) and some kinds of plastic.

Give each child a copy of the worksheet.
Make sure children understand the key. Then in turn discuss each material in the simple database. Show children an example of an object made from the material as you discuss it.

Elicit or give the children the following basic information **adding information about where local recycling facilities exist.**

Metal: Steel cans are sorted from aluminium cans by magnets (demonstrate that steel cans are attracted to the magnet and aluminium ones are not). The separated metals are crushed and taken to a factory where they are heated until they are so hot they melt. The hot metal is moulded into new shapes.

Glass: The bottles are taken to a factory. They are crushed into tiny pieces similar to sand and heated. They are heated until they are so hot they melt. The hot glass is moulded into new shapes.

Plastic: There are lots of different kinds of plastic. The ingredients used to make plastic have to be clean and pure. Some kinds of plastic can't be mixed in the recycling process. Most plastics do not biodegrade.

Paper: The paper recycling process is similar to the activity in Unit 11 but takes place in a factory. Large amounts of water are used and some 'new pulp' from shredded trees has to be added to the mix, making the new paper.

Show the children the cardboard drinks carton. Cut it open and show the children the layer of plastic or foil inside. Explain that objects made of more than one material are more difficult to recycle. **Stress that separating waste into different materials is an important way of reducing waste.**

Now make sure the children understand the questions on the worksheet. Let them complete it.

In the plenary discuss the children's answers, look at their poster designs and ask them why they designed their poster on the back of the worksheet. (The children are reusing the worksheet and reducing waste.)

Do we have to throw these materials away?

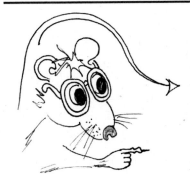

Here is a key.

The face will tell you if the material has these properties.

Yes	☺
Sometimes	😐
No	☹

Look at this database and answer the questions.

Material	Can it be recycled in factories?	Will the material biodegrade?
Materials that come from out of the ground		
Metal	☺	☹
Glass	☺	☹
Plastic	😐	☹
Materials that grow on plants or animals		
Paper	☺	☺

1. Which materials can definitely be recycled?

_____

_____

2. Which materials can be biodegraded to become food for plants?

_____

_____

_____

3. Why does a lot of plastic get thrown away?

_____

_____

_____

_____

_____

4. On the back of this worksheet design a poster.
   Persuade other children in your school to recycle materials.

Unit 16 Do we recycle enough?

OBJECTIVES

- To carry out a survey of how the families of children in the class treat different kinds of waste material and represent the data collected in a block graph.
- To encourage children to identify ways recycling performance can be improved.

MAIN IDEAS

A carefully structured class lesson where children collect and record information about the recycling habits of the families of children in the class. They think and discuss how recycling performance can be improved.

CLASS ACTIVITY

Resources needed
- Enlarged copy of the worksheet
- Coloured pencils
- Worksheet per child

Prior to the lesson: Cut out and paste the questionnaire at the foot of this page onto school headed notepaper. Make a photocopy for each child to take home and complete with one of the adults in their family.

Give out a copy of the questionnaire for each child to take home and complete with an adult. Explain how to complete the questionnaire. Tell the children when they will use the information.

In the lesson: Give out the worksheet. Tell the children that together they are going to complete a survey about how their families treat waste material.

Tell them to look at their completed questionnaire.

Tell the children that they must put up their hand and be counted for one option for each material, i.e. recycle most of the waste, recycle some of the waste, do not recycle this waste.

For each waste material, count the numbers for each option and record the totals in the appropriate cell on the enlarged worksheet.

Tell the children to fill in the same cells on their worksheet too.

As a demonstration, on the enlarged copy of the worksheet select colours for the key in question 2. Now, using the information from the survey, colour in appropriate blocks of cells in the *glass* section of the graph in question 3.

Show the children how the blocks of colour represent the three ways families deal with waste materials.

Let children complete the bar chart and collect in the completed questionnaires.

While the children complete the worksheet, fasten the questionnaires to appropriate surfaces around the room, so that children can read suggestions about how families can be helped to recycle more.

When the children complete the bar chart tell them to read some of the answers to the question, *what would help families to recycle more?* on the questionnaires. Then, tell the children to use the ideas they've read to complete the worksheet.

In the plenary, discuss the things that would help families to recycle more.

Dear Parents,
In school the children are completing a survey on the recycling of waste materials.
Please could you help them by putting a tick in the correct rectangles for your family?

	We recycle most of this waste	We recycle some of this waste	We don't recycle this waste
Glass bottles and jars			
Metal cans and tins			
Plastic bottles and containers			
Newspaper and magazines			

On the back of this paper, please would you list some ideas on how you think families can be helped to recycle more? Thanks for your help,

Yours sincerely

	Recycle most of this waste	Recycle some of this waste	Don't recycle this waste
Glass bottles and jars			
Metal cans and tins			
Plastic bottles & containers			
Newspaper and magazines			

1. Write the number of families in your class who treat their waste materials in each of these ways.

We recycle most of this waste.	
We recycle some of this waste	
We don't recycle this waste	

2. Choose three different colour pencils and colour this key.

3. Use your colours and numbers to make a bar chart to show how the families of children in the class treat the waste.

glass	
metal	
plastic	
paper	

4. What would you do to help families to recycle more?
Write your ideas on the back of this worksheet.

OBJECTIVES

- To consolidate children's understanding of what can be reused, recycled or biodegraded.
- For the children to devise a strategy for reducing the waste that goes to landfill or incineration from the classroom.

MAIN IDEAS

Using a key and acquired knowledge, the children identify common materials from classroom waste that can be reused, recycled or biodegraded.

They plan what facilities and rules are needed in the classroom to minimise 'absolute waste'.

CLASS ACTIVITY

Resources needed
- Orange peel, newspaper, plastic sweet wrapper, glass milk bottle, metal drinks can
- Enlarged copy of the worksheet
- A worksheet for each child
- Flipchart

Tell the children that at the end of this lesson they may be able to make their classroom a better place.

By questioning and answering revise and bring together the following information from previous units:

- Why do we need to stop wasting so many materials? Some materials are finite and will run out. Landfill sites are filling up and incineration can cause pollution.
- Why should we separate waste into different materials? Different materials can be recycled, reused or biodegraded.
- Which materials can be recycled? Paper, metal, glass, some plastics. Plants and animals can be biodegraded.
- What does 'biodegraded' mean? This is when animal and plant waste is eaten by worms and small creatures and changed into food for plants to grow. It is natural recycling.

Give the children a copy of the worksheet. Show them how to use 'smiling, neutral and frowning' faces to complete the table.

Tell the children that they are going to draw one of the faces in each rectangle in the table in question 1.

Draw their attention to the fourth column of this table, was it really needed? Explain that the meaning of this column is: did we really need to buy or use the object that is being thrown away in the first place? Tell the children there will not be correct answers to this question and to some of the others. However, you might ask them to explain their choice at the end of the lesson.

Tell the children to look at the table and think about the materials that are being thrown away in order to answer questions 2 and 3.

Let the children complete the worksheet.

Leave lots of time for the plenary session.

In it discuss the children's answers to table 1 and listen and comment positively on children's answers to the question: was it really needed?

Finally guide children through the final section. Draw up a code of conduct/set of 'rules' in children's terms that match the following sentences. Write them on a flipchart etc. for future use.

To stop waste from the classroom going to landfill or incineration the children need to:

1. Stop unnecessary waste coming into the classroom. Ask the simple question 'Do we need that stuff?'
2. Identify any items that can be reused.
3. Separate the other waste into different materials which in your locality can be recycled, biodegraded or discarded into landfill or incineration as 'absolute waste'.
4. Ensure that the waste is transferred from the classroom to the appropriate facility.
5. Monitor the 'absolute waste' destined for landfill or incineration and try to reduce it.
6. Tell everyone, pupils, teachers, caretakers, parents etc., who use the classroom what the class are doing and why!
7. Get on and do it.

OTHER ACTIVITIES

Once you've worked out what to do to reduce your classroom waste, the children can make poems, raps, songs, plays, posters etc. to spread the word!

Reduce
Reuse
Recycle
NOW

Here is a key.

Yes	
No	
Perhaps	

1. Use your key to complete this table.

The waste that is being thrown away.	Can it be reused?	Can it be recycled?	Will it biodegrade?	Was it really needed?
Orange peel				
Newspaper				
Plastic sweet wrapper				
Glass milk bottle				
Metal drinks can				

2. Which of the five things in the table probably has to go to the landfill site or incinerator?

3. How could you stop most of the waste from your classroom going to a landfill site or incinerator? (Write on the other side of the paper if you need more space.)

The strongest egg box competition

OBJECTIVES

- To plan a test to find out how strong an egg box is.
- To decide what evidence to collect, considering what evidence to collect, what to change, and what to measure.
- To design, build and test an egg box.
- To make comparisons and draw conclusions.
- To reuse and recycle materials

MAIN IDEAS

This unit should be fun. It is a structured lesson where the children decide on a test to apply to egg boxes made by the pupils.

Firstly there is a class discussion which agrees the task and method of testing. Children build their egg box from reusable waste objects. Then a supervised test takes place and comparisons and conclusions are drawn.

CLASS ACTIVITY

Resources needed

- A wide range of waste objects, e.g. newspaper, cardboard boxes, plastic bubble packaging, fabrics, plastic boxes and tubs etc.
- Masking tape, string, glues
- Commercial egg boxes as a visual aid
- Chalkboard/Flipchart
- One egg for each pair of children
- A copy of the worksheet per child
- A bucket

Tell the children you are going to have a competition. Show them the commercial egg boxes and tell them that:
- In pairs they are going to design and make a strong box to protect a single egg;
- Their egg boxes will take part in a test of strength. Ask the children what is a strong egg box?

There are at least three ways the children's egg boxes can be tested for strength:

1. Dropped without breaking an egg. If your school has an open staircase it might be possible to test the egg boxes by dropping them from the same height. Eggs that remain un-scarred can perhaps be dropped a second time from a point higher up the staircase!

2. Withstand a violent knock. In turn the egg boxes are put on a hard floor. Increasing weights are dropped from a fixed height above the egg down a cardboard tube. The tube guides the weights to the egg box target and prevents accidents to children.

3. Squashed by a heavy weight. Each egg box is put in the same place between the covers of a file paper folder. Weights are placed above the egg box on top of the folder until the egg box begins to collapse under pressure.

Now discuss with the children how they would devise a safe fair test for some of these possibilities. Guide the children appropriately and after the discussion select:
- **One** method of testing;
- What exactly they are going to test;
- What in the test will stay the same and what will change;
- Any other rules, such as permitted time and materials.

Give the pairs of children a fixed amount of time for the task. 15–20 minutes is probably sufficient for most children. Don't give out any eggs at this stage! Tell the children to make their container too big. They can put other packaging around the egg during the test. Having established the parameters of the test encourage divergent solutions, i.e. in one school, that tried dropping egg boxes from a height, the 'best' boxes were parachute assisted! These unusual solutions make the testing more fun. It also creates discussion opportunities in the plenary session.

As the children finish designing their egg box, give out the worksheet to each child. Tell them to complete the first activity.

Supervise and conduct the test.

Let children record on the worksheet the results of the test on each egg box.

If the eggs break during the test, manage the waste. Put the broken eggs in the bucket.

At the end of the test discuss the results with the children. Let them complete the last section on the worksheet.

In the plenary, listen to children's comments on how to improve the egg box and the test. Also look at the waste that the testing has produced. Identify:
- Materials that can still be reused.
- Materials that are waste. Use your classroom code of conduct/rules (from Unit 17) to manage the waste. Remember dirty card and paper, can all be composted. If your compost bin is enclosed and rat proof, the broken eggs can go in it. If not, bury them in a small hole in a garden and feed the worms!

The strongest egg box competition

1. Draw a picture of the egg box you designed.
   Explain why you used the materials you chose.

2. What were the results of the test?

Name	Score	Name	Score

3. Which egg box won and why?

_____

_____

_____

_____

4. On the back of the worksheet write how you could improve your egg box and improve the test.

Less rubbish in the classroom!

OBJECTIVES

For children to:
- Revise and understand the classroom strategy for reducing waste;
- Increase their awareness of how waste is produced or reduced.

MAIN IDEAS

This lesson is an activity based on a pupil's lunch box. It identifies the waste produced. The children are asked to design a lunch box with much less waste.

CLASS ACTIVITY

Resources needed
- Enlarged copy of the worksheet
- Empty containers and packaging similar to those on the worksheet
- Worksheet per child (note if waste is incinerated in your area amend the final column of the table on the worksheet).

Show and remind the children the 'classroom code of conduct for reducing waste' from Unit 17.

Tell the children that they are going to look at a lunch box. Tell them they are going to think about how they would treat the waste that is produced.

Give the children the worksheet and discuss the contents with them. Explain that in question 1 they need to create a key and colour in all of the 'what might happen to the rubbish boxes'. Show them how to colour the boxes for the 'Grape Plastic Bag' in ways that are appropriate for your school's situation, i.e. Reuse – perhaps, Recycle – No, (in most schools), Compost – No, Landfill – Yes (eventually).

Let them complete the worksheet.

In the plenary, discuss the waste produced by each of the items in the lunch box and what would happen to it. Encourage discussion but focus it on reducing waste.

Here are a few suggestions:
Plastic bag around the grapes It could be reused a few times but eventually it would need to be thrown away.

Plastic bags can be recycled. However, in most places they are not and go into landfill or incineration.
Grape stalks These are biodegradable and ought to be composted. They don't need to go to landfill.
Cardboard raisin box The box could be reused in the classroom for art etc. Card can be accepted in the community paper recycling bins in many areas. However, it can be shredded and added to the school compost heap. It definitely doesn't need to go to landfill.
Fruit juice carton Cut an empty carton open and show the children the hidden layers of plastic or foil. It is difficult to recycle because it is made of more than one material.

It could be adapted and reused as a flowerpot but eventually it will go to landfill.
Plastic yoghurt pot This could be reused in the classroom for art work. In some areas it may be recycled. In most areas it will go to landfill.
Metal foil around sandwiches This could be reused for wrapping sandwiches on other days. In many areas there are recycling facilities for aluminium foil. Some charities collect milk bottle tops etc. as the metal is very valuable.
Chocolate biscuit plastic wrapper, the crisp packet and the drinking straw. These plastic items are very difficult to recycle. The logistics of collection, storage and transport to recycling facilities is expensive compared to production from raw materials. They will almost certainly go to landfill.

Changing the lunch box contents

There are many ways that the waste brought to school can be reduced. Most of the items could be packaged into reusable containers, i.e. drink and sandwiches. Yoghurt, biscuits and crisps could be purchased in bulk and transferred to reusable containers too.

There would still be some packaging waste at home but less than for individual items.

Some of the items could be exchanged for similar things. Grapes could be swapped for either an apple, or an orange, which would need no packaging.

Crisps and chocolate biscuits could be exchanged for other confectionery items that could be packaged in paper bags, e.g. cakes.

Remember, there isn't a 'right' answer but raising awareness helps individuals make more informed choices.

Look at this lunch box.

1. If all of the food is eaten, work out what rubbish is left over. Write your answers in the table.

Now choose three colours

for a key: ☐ **Yes**

☐ **No**

☐ **Perhaps**

Colour in all the boxes to show what might happen to the rubbish.

Food	Rubbish left	Reuse	Recycle	Compost	Landfill
Grape	plastic bag				
Grape	stalk				
Raisins					
Fruit Juice					
Drinking straw					
Yoghurt					
Sandwiches					
Chocolate biscuit					
Crisps					

2. How would you change what goes into this lunch box so there is less waste left in your classroom? Write your ideas on the other side of this paper.

Sorting out the rubbish

OBJECTIVE

For children to:
• Revise and understand strategies for reducing waste.

MAIN IDEAS

This lesson consists of a class game and discussion and concludes with a revision activity. This will produce posters to inform other members of the school community of some of the ideas in this project.

CLASS ACTIVITY

Resources needed
• Cards on which is written an enlarged version of either a sentence **beginning** or **end** copied from the text below
• Blu Tack
• A hat
• Worksheet per child
• Chalkboard or white board
• Some examples of objects made from recycled materials
• Copy of worksheet 20 for each child
• Art materials for making posters

Tell the children that you're going to play a game that makes sense out of this project.

Put all the cards with ends of the sentences in the hat.

Now fasten each of the sentence beginnings on to the chalkboard or white board with Blu tack. Ask the children to suggest what appropriate sentence endings might be.

Let a child select one sentence end from the hat. With the children, identify the appropriate sentence beginning and fasten the end alongside it. Discuss:
• The reasons why each sentence makes sense;
• What will happen if we ignore the advice in the sentence?
List the children's ideas on the chalkboard or white board to help them when they complete the worksheet. Identify examples of materials or objects that fit the description as appropriate.

Don't buy things *that you don't really need*.
It wastes money.
It may help to use up materials that, sometime in the future, will run out.
The unneeded object will probably be thrown away and may help fill a landfill site or be incinerated.

Buy things that are made from materials *that have been recycled or that can be grown*.
Using recycled materials helps keep other materials either in the ground or growing. These unused materials can be used in the future. (Show the children some examples of objects made from recycled materials, e.g. containing recycled paper.)

Before you throw something away *try to find a way of reusing it*.
Reusing objects prevents them being dumped in landfill or going for incineration. It can save money and prevent materials being wasted.

Recycle waste materials *such as metal, glass and paper*.
This stops valuable materials being wasted. It prevents them from going to landfill or incineration. It can save money.

Try to separate biodegradable waste *and make sure it is turned into compost*.
Composting prevents the materials from being put in landfill sites or incinerators. Compost is a valuable food for plants.

Give each child a copy of the worksheet and discuss how they should complete it. Explain that the poster (activity 3) would contain:
• A small number of words so that it is easy to read;
• Drawings and pictures that help explain why the advice is a good idea.

Let the children complete the worksheet.

After a short while bring the children back together and discuss what they would put on their posters to persuade other people to follow each of the 'advice sentences'.

Then let the children make their posters on a separate sheet. Let the children see each other's designs in the plenary session.

Sentence beginning	Sentence end
Don't buy things	that you don't really need
Buy things that are made from materials	that have been recycled or that can be grown
Before you throw something away	try to find a way of reusing it
Recycle waste materials	such as metal, glass and paper
Try to separate biodegradable waste	and make sure it is turned into compost

1. Copy one of the sentences that was finished by words pulled out of the hat.

2. Why is the advice in this sentence such a good idea?

3. What would you put on a poster to persuade other people to follow this advice? Plan the words and drawings.

Where to get additional help

Information on rats and other mammals:
British Mammal Society
The Mammal Society
2B Inworth Street
London
SW11 3EP
Tel: 020 7350 2200
www.abdn.ac.uk/mammal/index

Details of composting, straw bale buildings, etc:
Centre for Alternative Technology
Machynlleth
Powys
SY20 9AZ
Tel: 01654 702 400
www.cat.org.uk

Purpose made tabletop wormery:
Insect Lore
PO Box 1420
Milton Keynes
MK19 6ZH
Tel: 01908 563338
www.insectlore.co.uk

Information on composting and compost bins:
Henry Doubleday Research Association
Ryton Organic Gardens
Coventry
CV8 3LG
Tel: 024 7630 3517
www.hdra.org.uk

Detailed information and well presented resources explaining the developments in the packaging industry to meet the needs of the environment:
The Industry Council for Packaging and the Environment
Tenterden House
Tenterden Street
London
W1R 9AH
www.incpen.org

Suppliers of purpose built compost bins and wormeries:
The Recycle Works
Unit W, Bee Mill
Ribchester
Longridge
PR3 3XJ
Tel: 01254 820088
www.recycleworks.co.uk

**Keep up to date on recycling.
Use the following websites:**
www.recycle-more.co.uk
Enter the postcode of your school to access the location of the nearest recycling facilities.

Materials

Plastic: www.recoup.org
Glass: www.britglass.co.uk.
Aluminium: www.alfed.co.uk
Steel (cans): wwwscrib.org
Paper: www.paper.org.uk

More information on energy from waste

www.efw.co.uk

More online information on Leptospira

The Weil's Disease Information Centre
www.caving.org/wdic

Other related titles from Southgate Publishers:

Green Shoots Series: *Learning about Life Cycles*
By Ian Mitchell and Allen Randall
Using a small organic garden to cover the learning objectives of the QCA Science 5B 'Life Cycle' unit.
Greener School Grounds
Learning through Landscapes
Teaching About Energy
Clare Eastland (TES Primary Schoolbook of the Year)

Wormery contacts:

District Councils
Most Local District councils sell wormeries at a subsidised rate, and in some cases free to schools.

Devon Worms
Higher Down Nursery
Mutterton
Cullompton
Devon
EX15 1RN
Tel: 01884 34248

Ecotopia
32 High Street
Stroud
Gloucestershire
GL5 1AJ
Tel: 01453 752345
Enquiries@ecotopia.co.uk
www.ecotopia.co.uk

Green Gardener
Jonathan Manners
1 Whitmore Wood
Rendlesham
Suffolk IP12 2US
Tel: 01394 420064
www.greengardener.co.uk

Original Organics Limited
Unit 9, Langlands Business Park
Uffculme
Devon EX15 3DA
Tel: 01884 841515
Fax: 01884 841717
e-mail: sales@originalorganics.co.uk
www.originalorganics.co.uk

The Bin Company (JK) Ltd
The Hawthorns, Oxhill Road
Tysoe
Warwickshire CV35 0SX
Tel: 0845 6023630
Fax: 01884 295303
e-mail: info@thebincompany.com
www.thebincompany.com

Westcountry Worms
Collaton Farm
Blackawton
Totnes, TQ9 7DW
Tel: 01803 712738
e-mail: info@westcountryworms.co.uk
www.westcountryworms.co.uk

Wiggly Wigglers
Lower Blakemere Farm
Blakemere
Herefordshire, HR2 9PX
Tel: 0800 216990 – Customer Service (free)
Tel: 01981 500391
Fax: 01981 500108
www.wigglywigglers.co.uk

Worms Direct UK
Drylands
Ulting,
Nr Maldon
Essex, CM9 6QS
Tel: 01245 381933
e-mail: enquiries@wormsdirect.co.uk
www.wormsdirect.co.uk

The Worm Hotel Ltd
Blythe Cottage
44 Littler Lane
Winsford, Cheshire,
CW7 2NF
Tel/fax: 01606 592145
www.thewormhotel.com

For construction of a cheap wormbin:
www.troubleatmill.com/wormbin.htm